The
ACCELERATED
JOB SEARCH

**For Job Seekers
With No Time to Waste**

Wayne D. Ford, Ph.D.

The Accelerated Job Search

by Wayne D. Ford, Ph.D.

Published by

The Management Advantage, Inc.
P.O. Box 3708
Walnut Creek, CA 94598-0708 USA

Printed in Canada

Copyright © 1999 by Wayne D. Ford

ISBN 1-879876-35-3

Library of Congress Catalog Card Number: 99-61114

Other Works by Wayne D. Ford

Books:

- Telemarketing Management for Business
- A Study of the Strategic Maintenance Process in Management Synergy Enhancement Programs
- Nursing Home Leadership
- The Salesperson's Stress Management Guide
- The Firefighter's Guide to Managing Stress
- Stress Management for Over-Achievers
- Managing Police Stress
- The Attorney's Guide to Stress Management
- How to Spot a Phony Resume
- The Ultimate Study Guide for Multiple Choice Tests
- How to Spot a Liar in a Job Interview

Audio Tape:

Stress Management Exercises on Tape

The Accelerated Job Search

TABLE OF CONTENTS

Dedication

This book is dedicated to my wife Kathryn, without whose patience, assistance, and love this book could not ever have been written.

The Accelerated Job Search

About the Author

Dr. Wayne Ford has worked and managed in numerous industries, accumulating over 30 years of management and supervisory experience. He has interviewed and hired hundreds of job applicants. His extensive experience as a full time professional career counselor and researcher has given him special insight into the job search phenomenon.

Along the way he has earned four college degrees, with majors of Education and Training Management, and Public Administration, as well as a Master of Business Administration (MBA), and a Ph.D. in Management. He has taught and lectured at the university level, as well as serving as President of a national training corporation. He has written and lectured extensively in the areas of business and organizational management and leadership, as well as healthcare, stress management, job search, and process sustainment.

He has managed a variety of organizations, including both single and multi-site, in the service, consulting, manufacturing, retail, sales, and governmental arenas. He has worked as a career developer and outplacement consultant, training job seekers in career directions, interview techniques, job finding, grooming, health, resume writing, and keeping the job long term.

He is married, has five grown children and a growing group of grandchildren. He makes his home in northern California.

Preface

The prospect of going into an extensive search for your next job is not normally something you would enjoy. What you enjoy is getting it over with. Getting through to the other side of the search into your next job is a goal you look forward to with some degree of anxiety and expectation.

This period of employment purgatory is somehow expected to be unpleasant, embarrassing, depressing, degrading, and, of course, too long. It does not have to be any of these things, least of all too long.

Over the years, while helping a wide variety of clients in their searches for employment, I conducted research on the various elements of the job search and found that conventional wisdom and standard methods resulted in far too much frustration, disappointment, and confusion. These methods also took way too long.

I tested a number of methods in an effort to find a way to shorten the process. I surveyed and interviewed folks in all areas of the hiring process, including human resource clerks, specialists, technicians and managers. I asked other career counselors, recruiters, employment agencies and hiring managers.

How were resumes screened? What was helpful, and what was harmful? How long did they take to screen a resume, and what did they look for? What kind of cover letters, thank you notes, and inquiries were effective? How should you dress for an interview? How should you prepare for interviews or assessment centers? A hundred other questions were asked of those who would know. I blended this with my own considerable experience in hiring, and I started coming up with answers.

In comparing the answers with what was being written and spoken as advice for job hunters, I was disappointed in the level of accuracy I found. Indeed, there was some good information being put out, and there still is; but overall I unfortunately found no single source of accurate, well-researched advice for the occupationally challenged.

For that reason I started putting together the information from my research and experience. My clients having been successfully using these methods, and it seemed to me natural that my 13th book should be on this subject. I hope you find it helpful.

Disclaimer

This book was designed and written to provide information in the area covered. It is sold with the understanding that neither the author nor publisher is engaged in rendering legal, accounting or other professional services by way of this book. If legal advice is desired, the services of competent legal counsel should be pursued.

Nothing in this book should be taken as the opinions or policies of any employer, associate, or contractor associated with the author in the past, present or future.

Job search is not a science and therefore has no absolutes. All information in this book is offered as an opinion of the author and should be taken as such and used with discretion by any reader.

The purpose of this work is to educate and entertain its readers. The author and publisher shall have no liability to any person or entity with respect to any loss or damage suffered or alleged to be suffered directly or indirectly by the information contained in this book.

If you do not wish to be bound by the above, you may return this book to the publisher for a full refund.

The Accelerated Job Search

Section One

Setting Your Compass

The Accelerated Job Search

Chapter

1

Why This Job Search
System Works

The Need for Speed

You are looking for a method to eliminate a prolonged period of unemployment and become quickly and happily hired into your next job. You have looked at books, read articles, heard of great career counselors, and been told a dozen sure-fire tips for getting a job. You may have been at this point before, and you remember how little fun it is.

You are fortunate at this time in having discovered this book. You now have the tools in front of you to use your time effectively and land your next job without wasting your time, resources, and energy.

OK, First Climb this Mountain

Are you still smarting from being told that the way to find a job is to throw out all the traditional ways of finding jobs and find the "hidden job market"? Have you tried "guerrilla tactics?" Have you "marketed yourself?" Have you tried the "inside" methods that are so *secret* that they are on the Internet?

Have you found that not only do these methods not work for you, but they waste precious time and energy? Perhaps you were told to try:

- Creating your own job.
- Cold calling on total strangers and asking if they have jobs.
- Using your "inside" contacts to get interviews .
- Finding a company you would like to work for; then finding the person who would hire a person with your talents, and ask that person for a job.

These methods are proven as having a very high success rate for job hunters who can use them. So what's wrong with using only these methods? Plenty. The reason is simply this : These methods work for some, but *may not work* for many job hunters, because their personalities and experience are not such that they are able to do these things. These methods are best for those sales-oriented professionals who naturally do this type of activity; but some folks cannot, so we cover other great methods also.

The Fountain of Truth

Many years ago, early in my career of advising clients on their careers, I advised clients to go forth and do these things exclusively (What was I thinking?) I quickly found that a high percentage of my clients smiled and said OK but did not do these things. A few did, but most did not. These were clients who were hard working professionals and strongly committed to finding a job. They certainly

19

were not the least bit lazy, and they faithfully followed through on every other thing that I suggested.

Then I looked at two other things. As a firm we administered the Myers-Briggs Type Indicator®. This highly effective, copyrighted test reveals a number of traits about people; including, after interpretation, what type of jobs and activities are associated with certain personality types. Both those who tested strong in the types that did well in sales as well as those who had experienced successful sales careers were able to go out and do these proactive techniques. They were in the minority, however; and after this discovery, I limited my advice in this area to sales types. To non-sales types, it is often as enjoyable and easy as walking over hot coals to attempt to follow these "secrets of finding jobs". It is not a lack of will, it is a fact of life.

The books that I have seen that push these sales-oriented techniques fail to mention that not all folks can do these things. It is often insinuated that job hunters that do not do these things are either not aware of them, are lazy, or cannot bring themselves to try something new. It looks great in print, but experience and research have shown me that this opinion is without merit. For sales types, it can have a measure of success. This book will concentrate on what will work for everyone, and *quickly*.

And Now, What *Will* Work, and Fast
(The SEEDS™ Method)

The great message of this book is how to use methods in plain sight better and faster and more effectively. None of the methods are "hidden", mysterious, difficult, or off the wall (or out of left field). There are no intensive classes, no secret handshakes, and no special passwords needed to use what you will learn in this book. What you will need is a positive attitude; a sense of commitment; a desire to work seriously at your job search, a willingness to use the tools offered to you; and some faith in the author that I know what I am talking about.

Once you learn and begin to accept and utilize the combined concepts of **SEEDS™**, you will gain new confidence. It stands for:

- **S**uperior tools
- **E**fficiency
- **E**ffectiveness
- **D**ynamism
- **S**peed

You will be able to not only to perform an accelerated and superior job search but to put this system to work on other projects both at work and in your personal life. Here is the basic outline of the system:

21

Superior Tools

The search, discovery, and use of job search tools that are superior to the standard will enable you to move ahead in your search and complete it faster. You will avoid much of the frustration of wasting time with tools that fail to assist you to maximize your efforts. Each tool you consider for use should be carefully examined to determine the extent to which it has been proven to help job seekers. Some of the superior tools included for your use in this book are:

- Attitude (Chapter 2)
- Career Directions (Chapter 3)
- Search Workplace (Chapter 5)
- Search Resource Protocol (Chapter 6)
- Master Application (Chapter 8)
- Resumes (Chapter 9)
- Practice Question List (Chapter 20)
- Cover Letters (Chapter 10)

Efficiency

Attaining the goals set out in the steps of your search plan on time, accurately, and as you had envisioned. This includes using your time in a manner which avoids waste and increases your chances of success. (Chapters 4, 5, 6, 7, 17, and 26)

Effectiveness

Using the process to achieve success in the different areas of the job search, including the attainment of the right job in the shortest period of time. (Chapters 1, 2, 3, 4, 16, and 17)

Dynamics

Maintaining a dynamic attitude throughout the job search and beyond. This includes priortizing, focus, and positive thinking. (Chapters 1, 2, 4, 7, 16, 22, 26, and 28.

Speed

Performing all functions without wasting time, and in an efficiently accelerated manner. Look for speed tips throughout the book like this:

Speed Tip #1

Eliminate postponements whenever possible. Make a habit of doing what is necessary without delays. Do it today, or even immediately if possible.

Do the Math

Is it worth it? Look at the average weekly pay for your next job. Multiply that by the number of weeks you will be unemployed. (OK, so guess.) That's the cash cost of being unemployed. It is money out of your pocket. What would you pay in money to shorten that period?

Let's take a woman who earns $52,000 a year, or $1,000 a week. If her search is shortened even by 3 weeks, what should she be willing to expend in money to make that happen? $500? $1,000? The answer is, of course, that any amount short of $3,000 is a net gain for her. If she is an average job seeker, this particular concept will escape her. She will: 1) Not consider the numbers, or she will: 2) Feel that a system that will accomplish this will either (a) not work or (b) will not work for her, or she will: 3) Feel that she can land a job fairly quickly using traditional methods.

When you do the math, you will find that the time and energy you expend in speeding up your search is a smart investment, paying off in rewards of money, stress reduction, and getting on with your career and your life

Chapter

Job Hunting With an Attitude

The Overlooked Key

The key difference between the average or standard job search and an all-out job search is the attitude of the job hunter. Attitude totally controls the intensity, personal resources, energy, time, creativity, confidence, and assertiveness that you, the job hunter, bring to bear in the search for employment. The control that you have is not immediately apparent to most job hunters, but you must *not only understand it but fully embrace it and use it*. It is a positive decision that you must make. Failure to decide this robs you of the opportunity to avail yourself of the widest selection of employment opportunities.

You may say that you are already determined to find the right job. That is a good start. You may say that you are highly motivated by a number of factors. That is also helpful. You may say that you have made a commitment to yourself and your family to obtain a truly worthy job with excellent compensation. Of course, this will be a positive factor. So what may still be missing?

Almost is not Good Enough

The missing key is the attitude that you will do what it takes, *whatever that may be*, to get satisfactorily employed. You may say that you are, but let's discuss that for a moment. In my practice helping clients to find employment over the years, I have run into a common roadblock. They would be willing to look for a job but only while staying within their comfort zones. Some of the more frequent statements I heard were:

- I'll do some of this, but I'm awfully busy.
- I've never been any good at that, but I'll do this.
- That never works for me.
- I know somebody who tried that and he had poor results.
- That doesn't sound like it would be helpful.
- I'd call, but I don't like to bother people.
- That's clerical, and I don't do that well.
- I could never be that organized.
- If I spend too much time on this stuff, I get depressed.
- I always seem to end up in the same kind of job.
- I certainly don't want to get obsessed about this.
- It's all so overwhelming.
- I'll try, but I can't guarantee I'll stick to it.
- This is not my style of obtaining a new position.
- People know I'm available. Something will come along.

Look at the list again. What these people are saying is that they will not do what it takes to find a job.   They will make an effort, and they will tell themselves and others they are job hunting; but they will not venture outside a comfort zone and try things that they are not comfortable doing.

Speed Tip #2

Eliminate needless roadblocks.   Do not trade short-term comfort for long term misery.   Only you know your own tricks for letting excuses slow you down.

I have told these folks something that may have been a shock to their systems: this is not the path to successful employment!   What a concept.   Actually putting forth maximum effort to gain one of the most important elements in your life.

Speed Tip #3

Make the maximum effort.   It will be leveraged many times by the reward of an earlier job start.

Attitude and Energy

The effects of positive and negative attitudes on energy levels can be dramatic as proven in many studies.   A negative attitude will drain off energy sharply, while a positive attitude will maintain higher levels of energy, all else being equal. You can see this effect quickly in your own environment. Those around you who are generally negative about things tend to be more fatigued and sick than those who are positive and "up" about events in their lives.

On realizing this, you can see that attitude can be an important help or a hindrance in your efforts to achieve the employment status you desire. Of course there is no magic wand to wave and thereby become more positive. It takes a commitment, practice, and an incentive. The incentive should be a happier life, and as a part of that a more successful job search can be an important element.

Speed Tip #4

Constantly practice being positive. The more you practice the more of a habit it will become and the more you can use it to create energy.

The attitude of those who consistently succeed is one not only of positive thinking but of *expecting to succeed*. This means going all out in all areas all the time. Going all out intermittently will not put you in front. Picking and choosing when and where you will give your best efforts is a campaign of personal convenience, not an all-out effort. It will not result in the best possible results in your job search.

29

Visualizing success and expecting to succeed keeps you focused on your job goal. See yourself in the type of job you want and keep that vision in front of you at all times during your quest.

Speed Tip #5

See yourself succeeding. Expect to succeed. You will work faster with the vision of success in front of you.

Constant reminders often help to keep levels of enthusiasm high. For this reason, you watch for and use the speed tip boxes throughout this book with reminders to keep your enthusiasm and positive attitude at full strength.

Chapter

Career Directions

Full Speed in Which Direction?

Landing the wrong job fast is not the fastest way to landing the right job. If this sounds obvious, then it would be a puzzle as to why so many people do it. So it is apparently not too obvious to lots of folks. It is often a question of inertia. "I hated the job and did not do well at it, but it's what I know, so I guess I'll do it again."

Thus we have millions of people moving from job to job, never finding happiness and job satisfaction. Unhappiness is explained away by these folks by pointing at hostile co-workers, evil bosses, unreasonable policies and procedures, unfriendly and uncaring employers, and just plain bad luck.

Some of these unhappy campers may actually identify the cause of unhappiness and include "wrong career" as one of their problems. But we hear that they have no choices. They are stuck by circumstances in this type of job, and there is no way out.

Speed Tip #6

Be sure you are headed in the right career direction. Starting over takes a lot longer than being careful at the start.

What About Bob?

Bob is typical. He got into banking right out of school and has been in banking now for over 20 years. He has never had a job outside banking. He has worked for three different banks and has risen to a salary level that allows him to support his family comfortably. His current bank has just merged with a larger bank, and his job has been eliminated. He has just started his job search and is only looking at jobs in banking. The problem is that he hates banking.

Bob feels that he is unable to look outside banking because he cannot support his family through an extensive period of re-education or re-training. Not only that, but he is unsure as to which different career he should pursue. He realizes that other jobs interest him, and he would love to try something else.

He assumes that skills he has acquired in banking are not transferable to another profession. He also assumes that skills he has picked up in hobbies, sports, and volunteer work as well as his natural skills and abilities are not being sought by employers in other fields.

What Bob needs to understand is that he is marketable in numerous other fields with little or no re-training. With some on-the-job training the field opens wider and with night school education taken while working during the day, the field is unlimited. Bob has many choices that he has not considered. With some enlightenment and counseling, Bob could do anything he wants to.

Speed Tip #7

Open your horizons. Not only will you see new opportunities, but your new awareness can attract opportunities to you, making your job search shorter.

You Must Find It

At a corporate breakfast I attended some years ago, I was privileged to hear a speaker who was at the top of his profession and whose opinion was sought by many on career success. He had failed in his chosen field for years by trying to do the job in a manner that most others did it. Multiple firings and intense frustration brought on depression and despair, but he kept on pursuing his career.

He finally discovered that the only way he could be successful was to do the job in his own unorthodox manner. Once he started to perform the job in the manner that he was skilled in, his success skyrocketed.

When asked by others how to achieve personal success, the speaker told them: "You must do two things, and you must do them at the same time. First, find out what you do, and do that. Second, find out what you don't do, and don't do that." This simple but all-powerful message encapsulates the most important career advice you may ever receive: Find work that you love and do well, and become employed doing that.

Speed Tip #8

Find out what you do, and do that. At the same time, find out what you don't do, and don't do that.

Accept no barrier, and overcome all obstacles in order to achieve this. Its accomplishment is worth nearly any sacrifice you may have to endure. The pain of being in the wrong profession is felt every day. If you are feeling it, do not let it continue. The everlasting punishment dealt to you without having committed a heinous crime is in itself a crime, and you are its victim.

To find one's place in this world is a noble quest but not always an easy or clear-cut path. Fields of endeavor which are attractive to us from the outside can turn out to be disastrous for us once we have chosen them and been exposed to the inside. The reverse is just as often the case, with evil and foul appearing occupations transformed to the job of our dreams when at last we gain the insight of their true nature.

An extensive process of determining your ideal job or jobs would (and does elsewhere) fill entire books and would easily do so here if there were space. It is not my intent to provide a complete and comprehensive course on finding your career direction.

It is my intent that you understand the importance of direction and that you have career options. Your job search speed will be disastrously impaired if you advance in the wrong direction. Within this limited space, then, we will explore career directions with the purpose of creating an awareness and better understanding of the process. It may be a confirming experience for those who are in a job they are fond of or an awakening as to possibilities for others.

Brain Surgery, Rocket Science, or Cab Driving?

The good news about setting out to find the "right" job is that there are many "right" jobs out there for you. You need only to find one of them. There are numerous ways to determine which of these would be a great occupation for you.

One way is to just start trying jobs until you find one you like. Although this is and has been tried so often it is considered a tradition, I do not recommend it. It can take decades and still not work.

Other methods include following suggestions from family and friends; taking aptitude tests and going after those occupations you score highest in (the military method); and reading through lists of occupations and choosing one that sounds good.

Assistance

If you want to get serious, use the services of a career center, career counselor, or other career assistance tool. What you want from them is to determine your interests and occupational suitability. Good ones will have excellent tests such as the Myers Briggs Type Indicator7 or similar instruments which can tell you about your personality and occupations that your personality type is compatible with.

They can also help determine interests and which occupations are compatible with your interests. You can also take these tests via the Internet. I do not specifically recommend any websites, but they are out there and available.

You will probably find that the strong point of many career counselors is helping you find your career field and sometimes on interviewing practice. Beyond that there is a wide difference in the type and quality of assistance you may encounter. Many are very good, while others are of less than optimum help.

I have been told by clients and have seen firsthand that while much assistance is good, not all career assistance is top quality. It is not the fault of the counselors, all of whom, I believe, want to help you. I feel that some lack training, experience, or natural ability. In this regard, it is no different than other professions. Like your search for a doctor or lawyer, if you feel you need one, ask around and get recommendations.

Ask the Woman Who Owns One

After obtaining your theoretical best jobs, go talk to those who are doing what you are focusing on. Do not contemplate this for a long time, just go talk to those doing the job and ask them. Who knows better? People generally like to talk about their careers. In most cases you will have no trouble in arranging an informational interview with an experienced person in the career field you are interested in. Some of the questions you may want to ask them are as follows:

- How did you get interested in the job?
- Did you always want to do this?
- Do you recommend it to others? To whom?
- Are you satisfied with your career? Why? Why not?
- What are the best and worst points about this job?
- Is there a future for this profession?
- What can I do to prepare for this job, should I choose it?

Speed Tip #9

When you need professional assistance, make sure you find a good counselor and then use what you can from those services. This can save valuable time.

Not an Excuse

For those readers who would use a search for career direction as an excuse (intentionally or otherwise) to procrastinate or slow down the job search: forget about it! Just the opposite should happen. Treat the career direction search as part of your overall career search.

The idea of finding your professional direction is an exciting thing to experience, and will provide you with increased excitement and energy. As in the rest of your search, throw your entire available energy into this part of the process; and use this energy to propel yourself forward even faster into your future career.

Section Two

Your Search Plan

The Accelerated Job Search

Chapter

Getting Your Mind Set

Your First Day on Your New Job of Job Search

Yes, you are employed. You are self-employed, and your duties are: research, communications, public relations, sales, correspondence, filing, morale maintenance, and much more. Unless you are still otherwise employed, this is your full time job. It is a temporary job, to be sure, and the more temporary the better, but it must be full time.

SPEED TIP #10
Start full time as soon as possible. Avoiding this is a major slowdown.

Many methods are used to avoid being in the status of job seeker. The equivalent descriptions of status are many, including:

- Unemployed
- Out of work
- In between jobs
- Occupationally challenged
- Displaced worker
- Downsized worker
- Laid off worker
- Not working
- In transition

- On sabbatical
- Doing a little consulting
- Putting together a few things
- Taking a breather from work
- Reassessing career options

There are many more, which as in the above, range from a status, title, or description of how you may be spending your time. Nearly all of them avoid the notion that you are aggressively searching for an outstanding job.

When taking one of these descriptions as your status, you are in denial of your need to quickly and happily become re-employed. This denial can be caused by pride, ego, embarrassment, fear, feeling overwhelmed, or possibly some degree of depression.

Taking the bold step of starting your new job of job search today can help to eliminate these barriers to becoming employed. You are the President of your job search venture. You call the shots. You say whether you are early or late for work; working too hard or too little; being productive or being lazy.

You can fool yourself on the surface but not inside, right? You can fool your family and friends, telling them how you are "busier now than when I was working" with lots of activities taking up your time.

45

You can talk about this company and that executive and that manager who want you to come to work for them.

You can talk of all sorts of imminent opportunities and possibilities, and this can make you feel better. Does it help or hurt your job search? It can nearly stop it cold in terms of real progress.

SPEED TIP #11

Don't believe your own excuses for not working at full speed and with commitment.

You must use the same production criteria as you would any other job. If you are not producing according to your master plan (Chapter 5), if you are not using SEEDS (Chapter 1) or other high production system, then you are not succeeding on your job.

The Announcement

To start in your new temporary job, you must announce it. You must, at a very minimum, tell yourself you are starting full-time job search and then actually start. To cement the decision, announce to others that you are starting full-time and that you have expectations of results.

Being responsible to someone is a large factor in every job. If you had a supervisor, then it would be that person. If you are the top person or run or own your own business, then it may be your customers. In any case, you are used to being responsible to someone for results.

For this reason you must establish the same thing on this job. Choose someone for your temporary job search mentor. The person does not have to supervise you, and in fact does not need to be a person who would or could supervise you. Just a person you can report progress to. It can be a spouse, parent, friend, or colleague. Just saying that you will be responsible to yourself is not as effective. This is not to say that you must report every action, but you must be responsible to this person for results.

Be careful in who you pick for this purpose. They need not spend a great deal of their time helping you in this way, but they *must care about you and your future*.

Speed Tip #12

Choose a job search mentor to report to. This will help you stay on track.

Tell the person you choose the results you expect to achieve and by when. Then set out to accomplish what you have committed to. Be totally honest with yourself and with the person you will report to. Otherwise, you are wasting their time and yours and sabotaging your entire effort. Incentive to achieve is provided by landing the job, but interim achievements are important also.

The mechanics of setting up and running your job search are covered in Chapter 5, but adjusting to the idea that you are employed at job search as your main professional function must be accomplished first. Starting the process before you have established your commitment will only imprint poor work habits and will slow you down.

Speed Tip #13

Commit to full effort before you begin. This avoids poor work habits, which slow you down.

The dynamics of maintaining full focus on your search full time will be a new concept. Do not think that it is easy, automatic, or that it comes naturally. It does not. The important thing to keep in mind as you start is that you *can* do it; and that with a positive attitude and the right tools and direction, you *will* do it.

Chapter

5

Your Master Plan

The Ultimate Time Waster

There is no greater time waster than disorganization. It is the opposite of organization, planning, and focus. It causes us to wander, to waste, to do the wrong things, to do the right things at the wrong time, and to do nothing. To achieve success in any endeavor without some degree of organization is not in the high range of probability. Obtaining your next job without first getting yourself organized into an effective job search will take much longer than it should.

Speed Tip #14

Before all, get organized. Do the right things, and do them first.

Putting an effective structure into your search does a number of positive things for you and your search including:

- Saves time
- Keeps you focused
- Helps to hold down excess actions and paperwork
- Helps you to be at appointments on time
- Shows you the big picture more easily

- Bolsters your morale and confidence
- Helps you to prioritize actions
- Keeps job search material from getting misplaced

Should you be an "organizationally challenged" or a naturally disorganized person, you should pay particular attention to this chapter. You may even want to enlist the help of another person to set you up in an efficient and effective system.

This may be especially helpful if this is the first time you have worked for yourself or the first time you have worked at home (if home is where your job search workstation will be).

Setting up Your Primary Workstation

If you are blessed to have an extra bedroom with a desk or a home office, then you may already have an idea as to where you will work. Although you do not have to work at your home, this is often the cheapest and most accessible.

Any good space will do, even the kitchen table, dining room, living room, bedroom, garage, workshop, attic, basement, space at a neighbor's home, a job club, or an actual office. Desirable qualities of the space would be that it is quiet, private, well lighted, and comfortable for you.

51

Speed Tip #15

Get set up quickly. Do not wait for equipment or supplies to be complete before starting.

Ideally you will have access to a telephone at the space and a good writing surface. Some other desirable equipment/furniture:

- Computer and printer
- Fax machine
- Copier
- Filing cabinet
- Desk
- Bulletin board
- Office chair

You do not want to go overboard in setting up an office or workspace. Not all the above items are necessary. After all, you do not want to be working here any longer than necessary. Getting too comfortable in this working environment could slow you down. Focus on the purpose of the space and be sure that it will accomplish that. Supplies and tools for your effort may include:

- Bond paper and envelopes
- Stapler

- Paper clips
- Pen/pencils
- File folders & labels
- Highlighter
- Legal pad
- Scissors
- Scotch tape

In other words, general office supplies. Again, do not go overboard on supplies. The above will probably be all you will need.

Try it Out

Once you get set up with a space, the equipment you will use, and a few supplies, try it out in your job of job search. You can make adjustments and improvements as you go along. If you find it absolutely is not working, do not hesitate to take dramatic action to change your workspace so that you can be effective. If there are distractions, too much noise, not enough room, or other problem, you need to solve it quickly and move on.

Prepare Your Appearance

An important part of preparing your workspace is preparing yourself. You must dress on this job in the type of attire in which you would attend an employment interview. If you are talking on the phone to a peer or a manager and you are dressed in casual clothing, it will come across over the phone.

We all have a picture of ourselves in our mind's eye. If we are sitting in our nightclothes or sweatsuit talking to someone whom we know is in a business suit, we will feel at a disadvantage, and it will show.

Your self image comes right across the telephone line as clearly as if you were talking in person. Take the time to dress and groom yourself in a professional image, just as if you were going to an important meeting. You will take yourself more seriously, and it will pay off.

Setting up Your Lists

Certain listings and forms will be important to your search and should be started right away. They will all grow and develop quickly as your search progresses and you add to them.

For those who do everything on computer, there are excellent contact management software programs available commercially which will provide much of the format you need. You can also maintain these lists and tools manually.

Ones that you will need include:

- Daily and Weekly Calendar
- Action Items (to do) Lists
- Resource List
- Contact List
- Target Listings
- Priority Protocol

Daily and Weekly Calendar

Many options are available to you, including portable daily planners, desk or wall calendars, electronic personal organizers, computer-based programs, or your own custom designed planning forms. It is important that you choose a format or system with which you are comfortable and can work quickly and effectively.

This single tool is what will keep you organized, on time, and working full time on your job search if you use it properly. If you are used to staying organized using a tool that works for you, by all means continue to use it.

Some adjustments may need to be made, especially if you will now expand or re-design your work day to include evening or weekend hours and off hours during a standard work day. The requirements of your search may include working hours different than what you are accustomed to. Many run into trouble here; because without careful planning and execution, you may end up working too many or too few hours for an optimum workday.

One example of many different styles.

18 TUESDAY	
Action List:	
Appointments:	

Speed Tip# 16

Schedule a breather periodically to keep from overworking and getting sick. This would definitely slow down your search.

Action Items (to do) Lists

This list consists of all the job search tasks you are planning to accomplish and is coordinated with your calendar. It can even be combined with your calendar as in the above example.

After prioritizing with a priority protocol, (see later in this chapter) you can create your action list and plug in tasks, meetings, appointments, interviews, and off time by time, duration, and place.

List more than just specific one-time tasks. List categories of activities, such as networking, internet search, research, informational interviewing, and letter writing.

List the approximate amount of time that you think that the activity will take, so that you can plan the specific hours of your day and week.

Example of Separate Action List.

On this type, you make your prioritized list, then check them off at right when you have plugged them into your calendar. Scheduled the highest priority items first.

Action List (Prioritized)	
Task	**Scheduled**
Schedule interview with Acme	☒
Call John F.	☒
Call Julie R.	☒
Send revised resume to RRR Company	☒
Pick up stationary	
Set up meeting with Carol	
Complete contact list	

Resource List

List here the resources you will be drawing on in your search. This is a good list to post at eye level in your workstation to constantly remind you of the assets you can access to speed up your search. At any given time, you want to be using your most effective resource to complete the task at hand.

Remember that resources are part of what keeps you from being isolated and working against the odds. Good resources can speed up your job search considerably.

Example

Resource	Contact	Phone
Acme Careers	J. Smith	555-1234
Library	T.Reader	555-4321
Industry Magazine	O.Boeing	555-4231
Job Club	I.Looktoo	555-9876

Speed Tip# 17

Post your resource list at an obvious place where you work on your search, so that you are always thinking of how to maximize it.

Contact Lists

This is your list of people who are instrumental in keeping your momentum and moving at high speed towards being hired. Types of contacts may include some on this partial list:

- Former colleagues
- Consultants in your industry
- Recruiters; internal and contract
- Former competitors
- Friends in related fields
- Career developers and counselors

59

- Hiring managers
- Human resource managers and technicians
- Industry association staff
- Chamber of commerce managers
- College and university career center workers
- Fellow job seekers

For each of these contacts, you need to quickly analyze the relationship to determine the type and extent of assistance the person will be to your search.

For some, one call may be the extent of the contact. For others, you may want to set up an informational interview to explore your career needs in depth; while with still others, a periodic meeting or phone call may be most effective.

Some contacts are helpful as references or as consultants to help you brush up on facts or details before an interview. A group of fellow job seekers can be an excellent support group to help you maintain morale, keep momentum, and share job leads.

Your contacts are the human element of your job search and can help you in many ways. They should be cultivated, appreciated, thanked, and rewarded in some way, when possible. A suitable reward is a sincere thanks and feedback that their assistance was helpful.

Example of Contact List

For your job search only, list the contact, the impact they have on your search, and access numbers.

CONTACT LIST

Contact	Impact, phone, E-mail
R. Jones	Reference
	(000) 555-1234
	RJONES@refnet.com
T. Smith	Consultant, recruiter
	(111) 555-7654
	TSMITH@connet.com

Priority Protocol

A priority protocol is simply a formula by which you determine the relative priority of tasks before you. This can be done in a number of ways, and we will look at two of the most common but effective ways here. Both methods use a combination of two factors: Importance and urgency.

The first method is to assign each task a numerical relative priority, such as 1 through 3, 1 through 5, or 1 through 10 or 15. Sub-formulas can be used, such as giving each task a number based on importance, such as 1 through 5, with 5 the most important. Then you factor in urgency, with factors of 1 through 3, with 3 being the most urgent. You then multiply the importance number by the urgency factor, giving you the priority number. Let's see how this would work.

Example

Using importance scale 1 to 5, urgency scale 1 to 3.

Task	Importance	x Urgency	= Priority #
Call recruiter A	3	1	3
Send resume to B	3	2	6
Set up resume file	1	1	1
Confirm interview with X Company	5	3	15
Review job ads	2	1	2
Pick up supplies	3	1	3
Call recruiter B	4	2	8

This example shows that the top priority task is to confirm the interview with the X Company, and the next highest is to call Recruiter B. The lowest priority is to set up a resume file. Setting up the resume file is easy, low stress, and you know how to do it. You may want to do it right away. The problem is that it is very low priority, and doing it now will block you from doing the highest priority task until you are finished. That would slow down your job search.

The second method is to place each task in importance categories of A, B, or C. Then, within each category, rank the tasks by urgency. Let's see how this would look.

Example

Using ABC importance categories and 1 to 5 in importance.

A Tasks	Urgency
Call John Smith	5
Send resume to Acme Company	4
Call for phone interview with Bob G.	4
Remind references to prepare to talk with XY Company.	2

B Tasks	Urgency
Set up lunch with Sue R.	3
Get plane tickets to San Diego	3
Search job websites	2
Buy new interview clothes	1

C Tasks	Urgency
Purge recruiter list	1
Pick up supplies	1
Review interview questions	1
Get bids on new personal stationary	1

After getting your priority listing of tasks before you, now list the amount of time that you estimate each will take. This is important to do before you start putting them into your calendar. If you have a lunch meeting at 12:00, it would not be advisable to start an important 2-hour project that you want to do in one session at 11:00.

Speed Tip# 18

Use your peak energy on your toughest tasks. If you are a morning person, that is where you should schedule the tough tasks.

Design it to Happen

Using these tools and others of your own, set up your master plan so that you can most easily and quickly make it happen. Use your energy and assets intelligently, putting your strongest assets against your most difficult tasks.

Chapter

Job Search Lead Sources

I'm Ready to Look, but Where?

Feel all dressed up with no where to go? When you get set up to start your search, your focus should be guided to a large degree on your sources of leads. The sources of leads to job openings and job possibilities are nearly limitless.

You will never be able to use them all, but then you do not need to. You actually have a dual role : find as many sources as you can and then narrow the leads down to usable numbers.

The main sources most often utilized in job searches include:

- Your own network
- Newspaper advertisements
- The internet
- Local libraries
- Industry groups and trade magazines
- State employment service
- School alumni career services
- Job clubs
- College and university career centers
- Internal and contract recruiters
- Chambers of commerce
- Job fairs

- Public and private personnel offices
- Employment agencies

Speed Tip #19

Prioritize your lead sources as you learn which ones are most productive. Do not waste time on unproductive sources.

Let's take a brief look at each of these common lead sources to see how they are used and how useful they may be to your search.

Your Own Network

Your network is made up of the totality of people you have met (in person or otherwise) and had interaction with. This includes your teachers, friends, bosses, customers, vendors, and all other persons in your life. Some will be helpful, while others will not or cannot. Do not be too quick to pass over some contacts who may not be obvious. Even your mail delivery person hears things.

List everyone you can think of, and then contact or eliminate each one. The ones who turn out to be useful contacts should then be put on your Contacts List. (See Chapter 5, Your Master Plan.)

67

Newspaper Advertisements

For many job seekers, this may be the main or only job lead source they ever strongly consider. It's a traditional source of jobs, so many "career experts" tend to downplay ads as ineffective. They give statistics to "prove" that you are wasting your time, and that other methods work far better.

Certainly you should not rely solely on the classifieds, but you cannot afford to ignore them either. They are an excellent source, and they should be used to their maximum. (See Chapter 14, Responding to Advertised Postings.)

The Internet

There are entire books on using the Internet to search for jobs; but if you locate and use a number of good websites, you should not need a book. There are many national, regional, and local sites that list all types of jobs, and on which you can post your resume. Many organizations, some of which you might wish to work for, have their own websites. There is usually a section for jobs.

The Internet is growing as a player in the recruiting and selection of job candidates. Some sites even use the newspaper ads as their data. This makes it easier to search by key word than it is when reading the paper version.

Local Libraries

Libraries contain much of the material you need to perform your search effectively. They also contain librarians, who can be of considerable assistance to you. Many useful directories reside in the house of books, such as:

- The Encyclopedia of Associations
- Standard & Poor's Register
- Directory of Executive Recruiters
- Hoover's Handbook of American Business
- Dunn & Bradstreet's Million Dollar Directory

And, of course, many more. The librarians can assist you as to which ones may be of the greatest assistance. The library may also carry trade magazines from industries you are interested in, as well as specialized books relating to the type of job you are seeking.

Industry Groups and Trade Magazines

Industry or trade associations in the industry you are targeting can be of considerable assistance in locating job openings, keeping you updated on industry developments, or in researching a company you are interested in. Many also publish a journal or magazine which is often loaded with information you can use.

State Employment Service

Called many different things in different areas, this is a governmental effort to keep employment rates high. It is a free service to help you find a job. Most have websites, and most have counselors, job clubs, and many, many job listings.

Jobs listed are at all levels and in all fields, even though many have an old leftover reputation of only listing dishwashers, laborers, and apprentices. Make this a definite part of your job search. The federal government (DOL) also sponsors America's Job Bank: http://www.ajb.dni.us/

School Alumni Career Services

If you are a college graduate, your alumni association may have assistance available in the form of networking opportunities, job opportunities in a newsletter, or an alumni roster, often showing where your fellow alums work. These services are usually informal.

Being a graduate (or even former attendee) of the same school as a hiring manager often helps in opening the door for an interview. Beyond getting the interview, the help tends to disappear; and you must get the job on your own merits. Since getting an interview is a major goal, this is a valuable resource if you have it.

Job Clubs

A wide variety of these organizations exists serving specific population groups and servicing a particular group's needs. Examples are:

- Teen job clubs
- Seniors job clubs
- Executive job clubs
- Re-entry job clubs
- New grad job clubs
- Welfare mothers job clubs
- Long term unemployed job clubs
- Industry specific job clubs
- State employment office job clubs

There are many more types of job clubs in existence, and they all have good things to offer. Most meet often, with some meeting 5 days a week.

Speed Tip# 20

If you join a job club, do not fall into the trap of transferring responsibility for your re-employment to the club. It is still your responsibility, and you need to maintain your own momentum.

College and University Career Centers

Most college career centers service both their own students and the general public, although the public is charged a fee. They feature testing of various types, individual counseling, and research resources, as well as job listings. They are cheaper than commercial career counselors and provide many of the same services.

Internal and Contract Recruiters

Internal recruiters with a specific organization recruit only for that organization. They may focus on one job class or group or may recruit for all positions within the organization. Their job is to help fill vacancies in their organization.

Contract recruiters (sometimes referred to as "head-hunters") are paid by employers to find top candidates for specific positions. They are paid in two ways: contingency and flat fee. The contingency recruiter gets paid only if a candidate they have found is hired. Flat fee recruiters get paid to conduct a search and to present the top candidates for employee selection. If the employer never selects a candidate, these recruiters still get paid.

Working with contract recruiters is somewhat different than dealing with internal recruiters. When communicating with an internal recruiter, you are talking directly to the employer, so caution is required as to what you say.

With contract recruiters, you can tell them more of your skills and background, because they need to "package" you for presentation to an employer. They know much more than you do what the employer is looking for, and so can select pertinent aspects of your experience to present and emphasize to the contracting employer.

Chambers of Commerce

The job of the chamber is to look out for the welfare of their members. This can include helping members to recruit qualified employees, so you can find job openings being posted by the chamber. Just remember they are working for the employer, and that's where their loyalties are.

Job Fairs

These events look physically a lot like trade shows and are even held in a lot of the same places. Some are small and are for one employer, but most feature many employers with booths staffed by recruiters or managers or personnel folks from the organization. Often hundreds of jobs are available, and you can ask questions of the organization's people in person.

Public and Private Personnel Offices

Larger organizations, including all levels of government have personnel or human resources departments staffed with specialists. They will have their jobs posted. Governmental offices (city, county, district, state, and federal) will often have positions from other governmental agencies on a clipboard or in a binder for their employees and the public to review.

Employment Agencies

The employment agency today is normally paid by the employer to find suitable candidates. Most arrangements are for temporary employment. Others are temporary which may turn into permanent status if both the employer and employee find the arrangement satisfactory.

If you go this route and get hired by the agency, remember you are an employee of the agency until/if you are employed by the contracting employer. These agencies usually specialize in certain industries and positions but will often also handle all types of jobs and can be found in the yellow pages.

Unsolicited Direct Mail

Occasionally you might receive position announcements unsolicited by direct mail. Your name may have been collected by a hiring authority from lists of licensees in a profession, from an association mailing list, or elsewhere.

Often these are positions that the employer is having trouble filling. Be cautious.

Recruiter Calls

You may get an unsolicited call from a recruiter who tells you that he or she is calling because you have an excellent reputation in the industry (a standard baloney line – don't get too flattered), and that there is this absolutely wonderful opportunity for a top person such as yourself.

These calls give an instant boost to the ego, and sometimes the opportunity truly is one that you could be interested in. Always ensure, however, that this is a position that you truly would be suitable for. The recruiter is trying to make money and please an employer.

Chapter

7

Health, a Key Element

Feel Great, Be Great

Trying to do your best when your body is lagging behind is tough going. So why do so many folks do so little to take good care of what they need for a good job search? The answer is that they are focusing on everything except their health. They are in a different, stressful situation, and it is more difficult to maintain healthy habits than it is when in a familiar more stable routine.

The stress and different conditions are not only poor excuses for poor health habits, *they are the very reasons to improve those habits*. We'll take a brief look at the key health elements to keep in mind so that you have your full energy to bring to bear on your search.

No attempt is made here to lay out a complete health program. There is sufficient help available in this area nearly everywhere you look. This is just a reminder on the high points.

You may be well aware of these health elements, but it can be quite different in the context of a search routine. You may tell yourself that you can ignore health habits for a short time, and then resume good habits when you are employed. This is a bad idea. You need your peak health for this time in your life.

Speed Tip# 21

Maintaining peak health and energy is crucial to maintaining the momentum of your job search. Consider it part of your job description.

Rest

Getting enough rest is not as easily done as you might think. Staying up later than you normally do can be justified by telling yourself you can just sleep later tomorrow morning and merely adjust your hours for a day or so.

The problem with this line of reasoning: your biological clock tends to not let you sleep much later than you normally do; and if you do, the altered sleep pattern results in low quality sleep.

Make every effort to sleep enough and to maintain regular hours. Getting by on too few hours of sleep takes its toll in one way or another. Some of the ways this happens are less obvious than others, but they will happen.

Speed Tip# 22

Don't cheat yourself on your sleep. It will slow you down by robbing you of energy, focus, and positive attitude.

Diet

Watch what you eat and especially *when* you eat it. Heavy and sweet foods can slow you down, so be careful not to consume them right before important events, such as contact meetings, key phone calls, and interviews.

While this is not the time to be overeating or putting on weight, it is not the time for a crash diet either. Extreme diets can leave you weak, disoriented, and lightheaded.

Exercise

Regular exercise is important; and as in the diet, extremes should be avoided. Don't sit around and do absolutely nothing, but don't start your training for the triathlon either.

Some regular exercise is better than none. Frequent short exercise breaks are better than 6 or 8 hours sitting and then a hard exercise period. Heavier exertion and aerobics helps the vascular system, as long as it is not overdone.

Exercising with someone else is helpful, assuming the person is about your same level in exercising exertion. Consider exercise a job duty, and maintain whatever you choose on a regular basis.

Stress Control

Excess stress drains energy and will slow down your job search from fatigue as well as fear of the unknown, feeling overwhelmed, embarrassment, depression, and other stressors. A strong positive attitude and maintaining other health factors will go a long way toward keeping excess stress under control.

A certain amount of stress is beneficial and will keep your search momentum going. It is *excess* stress that will lead to problems that will attack your bodily systems and retard or destroy your ability to pursue projects such as a job search.

A balanced lifestyle is essential to maintain controllable stress levels. Be sure that you do not ignore recreation and entertainment as part of a program of balance in your life. A quick study of stress and how it affects you is an excellent idea.

I would recommend my book: "Stress Management for Over-Achievers" to address stress factors during your job search. (How's that for a plug?) It's available from The Management Advantage, Inc. (888) 671-0404 or on the web at www.management-advantage.com where you can order this book, also.

Section Three

Creating Search Tools

The Accelerated Job Search

Chapter

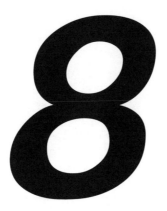

The Master Application

What, Who, Where, When, How, and Why?

You send your resume with a great cover letter to ABC Company, and you get a phone call to come in for an interview. You show up at the appointed place and time, and you are handed an employment application. "But I sent in a resume ." you say. "Yes we have that," smiles a nice young lady. " so if you'll complete the application, just hand it back to me, and I'll tell Mrs. Green who'll see you then."

Well, you may be surprised, irritated, or confused, but many organizations do exactly as described above. OK, you tell yourself, you will just fill it out quickly and get on with the interview. Then you see that this application form asks for dates, names, and other details that you do not have at your fingertips. It is a different animal than your resume , and you start to feel a little panic.

You ask the smiling young lady if you can get the rest of the information to her later. You know that it would be too late for the interview that way, but what can you do?

The smiling young lady stops smiling, and gives you that *what are you trying to pull?* look. "Just do the best you can." she says. You can almost hear her thinking: "Another idiot…."

Are you expected to have a photographic memory or carry all that data around with you? Frankly, yes. To be prepared for this situation you indeed do need to have data with you. You can list it in straight text or notes, or you can use a format similar to a typical application.

If using a form, you can use an existing employment application and then add what it does not cover. No application covers everything, although some seem to. There are one-page super simple forms, and then there are exhaustive "books" asking for your life's entire history in minute detail. This type is used more commonly where a security clearance is involved, or for sensitive government positions.

Gimme the Usual

The information you will most often be asked will include some from the following non-inclusive list: *(If you have this data you should be prepared)*

- Full name, including maiden names, previous married names, adopted names, and any other former names or nicknames you may have been known as.
- Current address and all former addresses, residences, post office boxes, military addresses,

whether rented, owned or stayed without payment, with exact dates.

- All home telephone numbers, current and perhaps 1 or 2 past numbers.
- Message phone number.
- Cell phone or other remote number.
- Pager number.
- E-Mail address.
- Website address, if any.
- FAX number.
- All driver's license and state identification card numbers, with class and expiration numbers.
- Social security number.
- Citizenship and U.S. residency status.
- Military service, including your branch, units, assignments, rank, dates of service, decorations, and types of discharges.
- All previous employers, including volunteer work, with address, phone number, and type of business, with exact dates worked and reasons for leaving.
- Previous supervisors, with current phone number.
- All previous titles and assignments, with descriptions of duties and responsibilities.
- Number of persons supervised.
- Committees worked on.
- Salary or commission amounts.
- Security clearances held, and type.
- Professional licenses held, with expiration dates.

- Professional designations.
- Professional association membership, with offices held and dates.
- Special knowledges, skills and abilities, especially as related to the position you are applying for.
- Languages spoken with level of understanding, speaking, and writing ability.
- All educational experiences and degrees, with names and addresses of institutions, and dates of attendance and graduation.
- Training programs attended and completed, with exact dates, providers, and course content.
- References, personal and professional, with names, titles, relationship, current address and phone number, and why this person would know about you, your skills, character, and competency.
- Computer competence, with specific application knowledge and experience.
- Any relatives working for the organization?

If you are thinking that this is an incredibly long list, it is. You probably will never see all these questions on one application; but you do not know which ones you will be asked, so it is then prudent to have all the information with you.

Preparation is the key to filling out an application properly. If you know in advance that you will need to fill out an application, then pick one up in advance and complete it at home, where you have the data and the time, and you can type it or very neatly print it.

Tough Stuff

The tough application questions were not included with the regular questions so that they could be discussed together here. The following can be tough questions if you are the focus of the intent behind the questions. Some of the tough ones to answer for certain applicants include:

- Why did you leave your last job?
- Have you ever been fired or asked to leave a position?
- Have you ever been convicted of a crime other than a minor traffic violation?
- Have you ever failed a drug test or used illegal drugs?
- Have you ever quit a job with no advance notice?

What to keep in mind about answering this type of question is: Never lie; stay positive and offer to give a short explanation; and never *ever* say anything negative about former organizations or management in order to justify your actions. It will backfire; painting you as someone who will speak ill about an employer. (See Chapter 19 – Tough Stuff)

Chapter

9

This Paper is You

Your resume totally represents you to prospective employers. It will not get you a job on its own, but it will help you get an interview. It can also keep you from getting the job if it is poorly constructed. Therefore, it should be as good a document as you can make it. It is all the employer can see of you.

Will You Stake Your Career on a Guess?

Advice on how to write resumes is available in many places and in many forms. Much of it is contradictory, and some of it is confusing. You can find it in books, in classes, in pamphlets, on the Internet, and from consultants, counselors, friends, and Uncle Joe.

Some books are nothing much more than copies of "successful" resumes. We must presume that this means that the presenters of these resumes were hired into the jobs they were seeking with that resume.

What we will never know is whether these folks would have been hired with a different resume; with no resume; or *in spite* of the resume. Some people are so obviously more qualified than other applicants that a resume written in crayon on a shopping bag would get them an interview.

Some years ago when I was laboring as an outplacement consultant, part of my function was to write a powerful, effective resume for each client. In my effort to produce the best product, I procured some of the best selling books on resume writing. I turned out resumes for clients based on the information in these books.

After a period of doing this, I became curious about the true effectiveness of the type of resume I was charging clients for. I checked the sources of the expertise expounded about resumes. All that was claimed was that these formats were "successful" in that they were used to obtain jobs.

I looked for surveys or academic studies purporting to prove the value or effectiveness of these formats. I could find two, and they relied, they said, totally on impressions of hiring readers only (HR, managers, etc.).

This is a better tactic than most, it's true, but as stated above, many applicants get jobs in spite of their resumes not because of them. The problem with surveying readers only is that they do not know what they do not know. They know what they like, but not how a graphic layout produces desired results. For this you need layout specialists.

To determine with a degree of accuracy if the more popular formats were effective in marketing my clients and procuring interest from hiring entities, I set out to conduct my own study. This study was not conducted with the intent of publishing the results but only to improve the effectiveness of my own resume writing efforts. This book represents the first release of the results of this study.

The Resume Study

The purpose of the study, then, was to determine which combination of the elements of format, content, emphasis, and style was most effective in causing the reader to take action in favor of the subject of the resume.

The questions to be answered were as follows:

- Who reads resumes?
- What are different readers looking for?
- How is a resume read?
- What helps, and why?
- What hurts, and why?
- What is the most effective format, and why?

There will make no attempt here to describe in great detail the methodology or process of the study; rather just enough information to explain the reasons for the results. The study was done with two groups of people:

(1) The most often readers of resumes and
(2) Advertising layout professionals.

The results were very clear as to what the most effective formats were as well as content.

Readers

The resume readers surveyed included:

- Human resource analysts
- Human resource technicians
- Human resource managers
- Human resource consultants
- Hiring managers
- Senior management
- Internal and independent recruiters
- Employment/staffing agency staff

These folks read resumes routinely as part of their jobs. Some of them scanned resumes at a fast rate to quickly select possible candidates and de-select

95

unsuitable candidates based on resumes and cover letters.

First they were given a list of questions asking: (partial question list, to give you an idea)

- What color of paper do you like to see?
- On what type of format do you find it easier to find data you are looking for? (choices were shown)
- What impresses you?
- What irritates you?
- What items would you like to see left off of resumes?
- Do you like to see dates of employment, or does it not matter?
- Do you read the writer's objective?

The rest of the questions were similar in probing the tactics, strategy, and working process of scanning resumes. The answers were tabulated and results were put into formulated protocols for use in resume writing.

Second the readers were given versions of resumes with the same data but put into different formats. They were asked to read these test resumes in the normal amount of time that they would take to read a resume on their job. This generally ranged from about 15 seconds to one minute. They were then asked questions about the contents of the resumes. The results were quite interesting, revealing that certain formats, wording, and content type were dramatically superior to others in getting key points across to readers.

Layout Professionals

The advertising layout professionals included graphic artists, copywriters, and layout specialists.

They were asked what they knew about:

- How the human eye naturally scans a page
- What type of format and wording directs and attracts a viewer's attention
- Blocks of type and white space
- Overall appearance

What they told me was also put into the formula and used with the survey results to develop the most effective resume format.

This is the important key so often left out. These professionals always focus on key words, sequence, placement, and general design. Just asking the readers what they are looking for gives you only part of the story.

Pointers

Pointers developed from studies and experience are presented here in the always and never format.

Some *Always* Points:

- **Always** use standard typefaces. They are easier to read by both human and electronic scanners.

- **Always** ensure 100% accuracy. A single typo, wrong word, or other mistake can give a chilling impression.

- **Always** use one page, unless you have a number of jobs and a lot to say about each one, then go to a maximum of two pages. This is a judgement call.

- **Always** use dates (month & year) for each job and educational experience. It gives a sense of credibility to the job, and readers like to see it.

- **Always** give a *short* job description for each job held – no more than 2 –3 lines. An exception would be a very technical description.

- **Always** list significant accomplishments at each job in bullet format. Short, beginning with an action verb. Start with the benefit of the accomplishment to the employer. This is eye-catching, and will be translated by the reader into possible benefits to the prospective employer.

- **Always** speak in the active sense, using action verbs. Tell what you actually *did*, never what you were *responsible for*.

- **Always** use a separate focused resume for each type of job applied for. This way you can list skills, knowledges, abilities, and accomplishments from your background which most closely relate to the position being applied for.

- **Always** use white or ivory paper. Readers tend not to like bright colored paper. They prefer a more conservative tone.

- **Always** lay out your resume with plenty of "white space"; never cramped and packed solidly together. This is far easier to read.

- **Always** include your e-mail address if you have one. More and more hiring managers like to communicate with it.

- **Always** list trade and professional association memberships if relevant to the position applied for. Include offices held if any.

99

- **Always** include a cover letter with the resume to make a case for your employment, explain any needed details, and ask for an interview. (See Chapter 10)

- **Always** proofread the resume and cover letter for accuracy. Have another person proofread it for further insurance. Spelling errors can be fatal.

- **Always** bring a copy of your resume and cover letter, a list of references, and a copy of a completed application, if that has been submitted, to the interview.

- **Always** ensure you have documentary evidence of all education. This can be degrees, diplomas, transcripts, or certificates.

Some *Never* Points:

- **Never** use fancy typefaces, italics, underline or graphics. This is harder to read quickly, and can come out of an electronic scanner as "garbage", or something that looks like %&##@*^)+=.

- **Never** use an "objective". Readers tend to ignore them, so they take up valuable space. They can even harm you if you describe something that does

not match the wording that the reader is thinking.
Many "experts" do not know this and will insist on
including it. Put this type of information in your
cover letter. Remember, an objective statement is
what *you* want; and you need to focus on what the
employer wants.

- **Never** state "references available on request" or list
  references. It is assumed by readers that you have
  references. It takes up valuable space.

- **Never** list hobbies or social activities, religious or
  political information. It does not help you and
  could hurt you. You may list something the reader
  finds distasteful.

- **Never** give salary information on a resume . If you
  are forced, include it in the cover letter.

- **Never** give health or medical information.

- **Never** give family information.

- **Never** never *never* lie.

- **Never** give your social security number, driver's
  license number or taxpayer ID number on a
  resume. This is not an application form. If
  required, put it in the cover letter.

101

- **Never** give a reason for leaving a previous position. This can be discussed later and should always be positive.

- **Never** explain gaps in employment in the resume. It is better to show "self-employed" or a similar listing if required.

- **Never** list arrests, recovery, or treatment programs.

- **Never** list the phone number of your current employer or supervisor unless you have notified them of your job search.

- **Never** use unexplained "buzz words" or jargon that would only be understood by someone in the field unless you are sure that no lay persons will read the resume.

- **Never** leave out part-time or volunteer work *if it is relevant*, but indicate its status as such.

Style

Readers most often prefer a traditional, simple, easy to read style, with an open, non-cluttered look. Massive blocks of type are difficult to scan and may not be read by a reader in a hurry.

Styles not generally preferred are simple lists of skills and abilities; a "qualifications brief"; or a general discussion of the types of employers worked for and duties with no dates or attribution.

Readers say they like a chronological resume showing what you did and where you did it. This is easy to read and digest quickly.

Types of Resumes

There are many types of resumes, including massive Curriculum Vitaes, or C.V.s, often used for teaching positions, which can easily span 20 or 30 pages for an experienced professor.

There is the Letter Resume, which is written in the form of a business letter; the Qualifications Resume, listing only skills and education; and many more. Based on primary research, I recommend a very traditional and straightforward type, which I cover in this chapter.

The Five Parts of Your Resume

Parts of the resume should be distinct and in a definite order. The five parts and their order are as follows:

1. The Heading
2. Descriptive Statement
3. Skill Summary
4. Work Experience
5. Education, Associations, Awards, and Special Accomplishments

The Heading

This should include your name in slightly larger type (no nicknames), with any relevant designation or degree, such as a masters level or higher college degree or professional designation (MBA, Ph.D., PE, RN, MFCC, etc.). Your address should be a street address, rather than a post office box number.

Descriptive Statement

Next, where many would place an objective statement, place a short, one or two line thumbnail statement describing the object of the resume. Examples:

- A highly experienced professional engineer with a wide breadth of project management and bridge reinforcement expertise.

- A reliable and competent bookkeeping professional with extensive experience in complex accounts receivable and billing programs.

- Introducing a consummate legal practitioner with a record of successful litigation in consumer affairs spanning eighteen years.

- One of New York's most accomplished writers in the field of molecular botany.

- A hard working, loyal, and reliable food service worker specializing in large volume restaurant lunch and dinner meals.

Yes, you are bragging, and this is where you should. This sets the tone of the *benefit* you will be to the employer. A counselor, early in my career, once told me: "If you won't ring your own bell, no one else will either."

Skill Summary

A bulleted summary of skills, by subject, clearly and quickly lays out your most prominent key skills. This is the most powerful part of the entire resume. Readers say that they go straight to this section looking for the nuggets that will help them.

Examples: (no more than four general areas.)

- **Computers.** Full knowledge of general office PC operations, MS Office, Lotus, Pagemaker, and other spreadsheet and database programs.

- **Supervision.** Hiring, coaching, orientation, appraisal, training, teambuilding, scheduling and disciplinary actions.

- **Food Preparation.** Purchasing, menu planning, entrée preparation, desserts, sauces, pastries, large and small volume, and banquets.

- **Construction.** Carpentry, electrical, plumbing, grading, roofing, and finish work.

- **Project Management.** Concept and strategy, planning, team formation, customer liaison, quality control, and outcomes management.

- **Sales.** Cold calling, prospect and territory development, presentations, closing, follow-up, and customer service.

- **Landscaping.** Grading, planning, planting, pruning, fertilizing, inorganic ground cover, concrete work, decks, and overall maintenance.

- **Bookkeeping.** A/R and A/P, general ledger, posting, reconciliation, filing, and operation of dedicated accounting systems.

- **Customer Service.** Cashier, customer complaint resolution, product location, packaging, credit determination, and repeat sales generation.

Showing three or four areas, as above with specifics, lets the reader see right away the skills you have that the reader can use.

Work Experience

Readers look at your work experience as evidence that you have performed certain tasks. They relate this reported performance to your future capability to perform similar tasks for their organization. This means that you must put the right information in the right place and in the right format, so that they may see it and understand it at high speed.

Think benefits. Benefits to the reader's organization that can be spotted by fast scanning. For each job start with the employer and the dates you were there, followed by a job description and bulleted accomplishments. Both the job description and accomplishments should be proactive.

107

A one or two line job description is best. It says basically what you did.
Example:

"Supervised all engineers in professional operations, represented the organization in all negotiations, and generated reports and analyses."

The strong point is that it used three action verbs: supervised, represented, and generated. These are power points. A weak, passive version would say:

"Was responsible for professional operations, negotiations, and reports."

The weak point is that it does not say that you actually *did* anything. "Was responsible for" is a passive statement. You probably know people that were or are responsible for things but never did them.

Next are the accomplishments (I like to call them "heroics") that you had while you were on that job. Many of my clients objected at this point saying that they never did anything out of the ordinary or made any significant accomplishments. A careful review always showed that indeed they did do significant things. If you worked hard all day and did a good job, then at the minimum you "avoided significant loss of productivity by maintaining high standards of work quantity and quality." Think about it. Any positive action you took or results you achieved can be stated as an accomplishment.

These should be listed by bullets under the job description. This is the best and easiest place for readers to pick them up when scanning. Start each one with a powerful action verb. This pulls the reader in. A few good ones among the hundreds of good ones:

- Achieved
- Adapted
- Arranged
- Authored
- Built
- Changed
- Conducted
- Coordinated
- Crafted
- Created
- Decreased
- Designed
- Enlarged
- Expanded
- Expedited
- Increased
- Initiated

- Instructed
- Invented
- Made
- Managed
- Operated
- Organized
- Persuaded
- Saved
- Set up
- Sold
- Started
- Produced

Put a strong benefit at the start of the bulleted accomplishment. Mention any strong point up front. Dollar savings or earnings, what was increased or decreased, improved or created. Then say how you did that. This conforms with the scanning dynamics of readers, whose glance runs down through the first 3 or 4 words of each bullet. If you have nothing there, you have lost the battle.

Good examples:

- Saved $30,000 by rearranging the operations scheduling.
- Created 20% increase in sales by writing and printing new brochure.

Not as good:

- Responsible for rearranging the operations scheduling, which saved $30,000.

On the first example, the reader's eye would be snagged by the "Saved $30,000", and the reader would be pulled into reading the whole bullet. On the second example, the first words were: "Responsible for rearranging" – boring. The reader's glance would move on quickly, likely missing the part about saving $30,000.

Other good examples:

- Improved morale by remodeling the break room.
- Increased revenues $15,000 annually by adding new product line.
- Saved 22 man-hours per week by automating the XYZ process.
- Increased flexibility of the team by becoming cross-trained.
- Decreased cycle-time of stamping process by creating special tools.

This format proved more successful than any other, making use of all the factors of what the readers wanted, needed, and liked as well as the scanning dynamics.

Education, Associations, Publications and Other Qualifications

This section is where you list: (With organizations and dates)

- Degrees
- Training courses
- Articles and books written
- Professional licenses and designations related to the job
- Professional association membership related to the job
- Special awards (Woman of the Year, etc.)
- Any special qualifications or similar *positive* facts.

Remember, include no personal, hobby, religious, family, unrelated facts or details in this section.

Resume Example

Following on the next page is an example of the resume format that tested best in extensive testing using professional resume readers.

Thomas Jobber

3456 Elm Street
Townsville, VT 00936
(101) 555-1234

A highly reliable widget polishing professional with strong technical and administrative skills

Skills

- **Widget Knowledge**. Concept, casting, grinding, polishing, materials acquisition, design, and effectiveness.
- **Administration**. Planning, scheduling, purchasing, record keeping, supervision, and business operation.
- **Customer Service**. Sales, follow-up, problem resolution, corrections, and repairs.

Experience

4/95 – Present   International Widgets, Townsville, VT
Chief Polisher
Full supervision of all polishing operations, sales and service. Staff of 45 polishers, 4 admin and sales.
- Increased polishing volume 45% by creating new process and training staff.
- Cut costs $14,000 per year with new process.

1/88 – 4/95   Acme Widgets, Vemotte, NY
Polisher
Performed all duties of journeyman polisher.
- Set efficiency record for polishing.

Education and Training

1987   Widget Polishing Institute, Burns, OH
BS, Widget Polishing

Type Will Dictate Length

The type of resume and the number of jobs will dictate the length of not only the entire resume but each job description, accomplishment, and skill description. Longer and more varied careers will require two pages.

Chapter

10

Cover Letters

A Documentary Chaperone

Much as a young lady in earlier times was not allowed to meet a young gentleman without a suitable chaperone to ensure all things went well, your resume should not be allowed to meet an employer without a cover letter.

You want to not only influence how the reader starts to consider you, but also how the reader looks at your accompanying resume.

You cannot assume that your resume is the only document that the reader will pay any attention to. It is a myth that the only purpose of a cover letter is to indicate which job you are applying for. Failing to include a cover letter is a big mistake. The second biggest mistake is to write and attach a minimal, poorly written, or misguided cover letter.

The first impression you make on your prospective employer is your cover letter. Why would you neglect an opportunity to make a good first impression on the person who could change your life? (You only have one chance at a first impression.)

Being polite, businesslike and brief to save the reader's valuable time may sound logical; but in reality it may shoot you down before you even get started.

A "standard" start goes something like this: "This is in response to your ad for a Cabinet Maker. I think you can see that I am qualified." This does nothing to help the reader see why she or he should want to call you for an interview. You need much more.

Purpose

Your cover letter must tell the reader why you are the person that can do the job and why. It must capture their imagination and convince them that in you they have a strong candidate to fill the position. This person should see enough to make them want to look at your resume for the structured backup information upon which you have based your letter. The letter clarifies and strengthens the resume and gives logical and emotional reasons for them to strongly consider you as a candidate.

Sorry, Wrong Number

Writing the letter for the wrong job or for the wrong reasons not only will waste your time and the reader's, it will tend to irritate them. Unfortunately this happens a lot. Writing about qualifications or skills in the wrong area is a quick ticket to the wastebasket.

117

Pay Attention and Shoot Straight

To some degree, employers will make it known what qualifications they are looking for. In an advertisement, job listing, or job description, certain qualifications will usually be listed. Some give extensive information on what they are looking for. If specifics are not given, estimate from your own knowledge and experience what qualifications would be needed.

Your letter should clearly state, point by point, how you meet or exceed every qualification. You can give equivalent qualifications if that is what you have, but the point is to *address each point*. Do not make the reader dig, search, or guess.

Be as specific and accurate as you can. If the qualification is stated as "ability to overhaul Acme B-25 Compressors", you should state that specific ability not "compressor overhaul experience".

Avoid lumping together qualifications if you can be exact. The stated requirements may be for five or six areas of sales management. Address each one instead of: "experienced in all areas of sales management." This makes you appear either lazy or lacking in one or more areas.

Grab 'em and Hold 'em

Start the letter with a powerful phrase or sentence that will grab their attention, then hold it by providing the information that reinforces the initial statement. If you start with a statement about your skill at increasing sales, then you should provide examples as to when and where you have increased sales and by how much.

If you begin by telling about your success as a construction manager, then you need to follow up by giving instances where you experienced this success and how it benefited your employer or customer.

This is the old promise-and-deliver technique. It works well in cover letters and can be worked into interviews as well. (See Chapter 17 on Interviewing Concepts) The promise gets their attention and sparks curiosity as to the when, where, and how of the evidence that you have done it before and can fulfill your promise to do it again.

Examples of opening statements:

- For fourteen years I have been building my experience to prepare for a position such as the one for which you are recruiting.

- My successful career in process engineering has given me a competitive edge in the industry and a strong enthusiasm for my work.

- Proven success in managing large manufacturing plants, product divisions, and owned manufacturing subsidiaries has made me a skilled manager and team builder.

- Your stated requirements are all areas in which I have extensive experience and continuing enthusiasm. My qualifications also extend into unstated requirements for such a position.

- The position for which you are recruiting is the next natural step in my career. You will find that I am not only qualified, enthusiastic, and well-recommended but fit in naturally to the type of position that challenges me and rewards me.

Refer to the bulleted accomplishments in your resume for your material on instances in support of your initial cover letter statement. This gives consistency and credibility to the combination of letter and resume.

Stating the same achievement or experience in both the resume and cover letter is all right, just try to re-phrase it a bit.

Examples of bulleted accomplishments by area:

Accomplishment Statement 1

My experience in expanding sales territories is extensive:

- At Ajax Products, I expanded the territory from Dallas/Ft. Worth to all of Texas, New Mexico and Oklahoma. Volume increased 450% in 2 years.
- At Superior Widgets, my territory was initially Los Angeles. Over three years, I expanded the effective sales territory to all of southern California.
- While employed by New Horizons Widget Associates, I coached four associates under my supervision who all expanded their territories significantly.

Accomplishment Statement 2

Evidence of my training management experience includes:

- As Training Manager at the City of Milldodd, I hired and trained a staff of four and established a training center and a full program of training courses.
- While at the Walker Company, my achievements included the building of a training team, creating a

learning curriculum, and increasing the level of production through specialized training programs.

- A lowering of cycle time and production costs was a direct result of my training team's courses for production workers when I was Training Coordinator for Southern Machine Products.

Accomplishment Statement 3

My experience at lowering costs in a maintenance environment can be seen by these examples:

- At Diamond Glow Facilities, I negotiated a purchase of disinfectant, which saved over $15,000 per year over previous costs for three years.
- Also at Diamond Glow, I re-wrote the scheduling policy for maintenance personnel, which lowered overtime costs $23,500 per year while raising morale.
- Eliminating contract landscaping and initiating an internal landscaping crew saved Seymour Materials over $44,000 per year and earned me an efficiency award.

Accomplishment Statement 4

My office management skills can be demonstrated by the following achievements.

- Phone coverage was improved at Lincoln Corporation, lowering answering response time from four rings to one by my re-training of office staff on phone procedures.
- I improved the accuracy and turnaround speed of legal report transcriptions by implementing an automated system and training staff in its use at Universal Law Center.
- Turnover in office staff was lowered by 25% when I increased morale at Acme Mobile Telephone. I did this by implementing personal recognition, career development, and individual coaching programs.

Positive Logic

After showing the points demonstrating how you have previously achieved or learned things that relate to the position applied for, tell how the logic of this would make you an excellent candidate.

Examples of logic statements:

- With the extent of matching qualifications, experience, and skills, I would appear to be a strong candidate for the position and would very much like to pursue my consideration.
- As you can see, I have experience which meets and exceeds the stated requirements for the position.

Ask for the Interview

Finally, after introducing your resume and position qualification specifics, you have said why you are a strong candidate. You now need to ask for an interview to move on to the next step toward your selection for the position.

Examples of interview request statements:

- It would be a pleasure to discuss with you how I could contribute to your organizational goals. I am available at any time to meet with you.
- I would very much like to discuss in detail the possibility of my joining your team there at XYZ Company. Please call me at (555) 555-5555 to arrange a personal interview.
- I believe a personal interview would allow us both to explore the possibility of pursuing my employment. Please call me at my home at (333) 333-3333.

Indication of Attachment of Resume

Somewhere you need to indicate that your resume is attached. Your letter may become separated from the resume, and you do not want someone to think that the letter was sent *instead* of a resume. A simple enclosure notation as shown below will suffice if not noted elsewhere:

Encl.: Resume

Completed Letter Examples

Using all the pieces, it is then time to construct the actual letter. An example of a letter using composites of elements is shown on the next page.

The Accelerated Job Search

Mary Jobmore
1234 Jones Avenue
Alltown, CA 95555
(555) 555-1234

May 22, 2001

Hiring Company,
ATTN: Joe Thornton, HR Manager
77 Sunset Strip
Notown, CA 95554

Dear Mr. Thornton:

My proven success as an office manager over the last 12 years gives me a considerable body of knowledge and skills relative to the position you offer. Specific points to consider from my experience:

- Phone coverage was improved at Lincoln Corporation, lowering answering time from four rings to one by my re-training of office staff on phone procedures.
- I improved the accuracy and turnaround speed of legal report transcriptions by implementing an automated system and training staff in its use at Universal Law Center.
- Turnover in office staff was lowered by 25% when I increased morale at Acme Mobile Telephone. I did this by implementing personal recognition, career development, and individual coaching.

With the extent of matching qualifications, experience, and skills, I would appear to be a strong candidate for the position ,. It would be a pleasure to discuss with you how I could contribute to your organizational goals. I am available at any time to meet with you. Your consideration is very much appreciated.

Sincerely,

Mary Jobmore

Encl.: Resume

Chapter

11

References

The Human Backup for Your Resume

The hiring authority sees your paper evidence of suitability and then sees you. All this information comes from you. Talking to a real live person is a much more powerful and credible indication of what type of candidate you are. Choosing those individuals who will be willing to speak well of you is an important decision. You are putting your future in the hands of these people.

For clarity, we are not considering a straightforward employment check with a previous employer to verify title and dates of employment. These are not the types of references under discussion in this chapter.

Once you have given the names of the references to the employer and the employer calls the reference, you have no control or influence over what happens next. Major surprises happen routinely.

Who Should You Choose?

The choice of what persons to give as references is not always as obvious as it may seem. Some employers will give you their parameters as to the type of references they want. Typical instructions may include:

- Immediate supervisors only
- Supervisors or co-workers
- Any co-worker
- No subordinates
- No relatives
- Anyone (no guidance or restrictions)

Obviously they would not be impressed by glowing references from your mom and from Uncle Harry. Other employers may state something like "References from persons who know about your character and/or work history."

Some may ask for 2, 3, or even 5 references. If the request is for a supervisor and not for an "immediate" supervisor, you are open to use anyone in your upward chain of command, a project supervisor or even staff supervisor. Pick the best one.

As you go over the list of who might make good references, you quite clearly want to eliminate persons with whom you did not get along with, who did not like you for some reason or would have a reason to say something negative about you. Be aware that merely because you got along with someone on the job does not mean they will say good things about you or put you in a good light.

Preparation

A reference can be misunderstood; can harbor unknown resentments; can forget who you are; can confuse you with someone else; or can be having a bad day when called. For these reasons, you need to contact your references and talk to them before giving their names as references.

Even if you are in current contact with former associates, you should never assume that they are automatically your friend and supporter. They may remember your work experiences differently than you do or differently than you have told the hiring employer either in your resume or in the interview.

The prudent action is to call them or see them and ask if it is alright (or still alright if they have previously given permission) to give their names as references. Tell them about the job or types of jobs you are applying for. Tell them what you are telling employers about your background as it relates to their own knowledge. It is nice to be on the same page with your reference.

You may have known a person in one context, perhaps day to day work, when you were at a certain company, and you have told the employer about what you did on project teams. Your reference here may have no knowledge of your project work and may say so to the employer. You could have a disaster on your hands. This is not a rare occurrence in the world of references. It happens quite often and delivers surprises where they are definitely not needed.

At the very start of your job search, call all those you may want to use as references and establish contact. When the time comes when you definitely plan to use them as references, call them again and give them specific details.

Quotes

During the interview process (Chapter 17), you may want to quote something that a reference said in your past experience together. A statement such as: "You are the most reliable worker I've ever had." is a powerful statement. The problem could be that your reference, perhaps a former supervisor, may not remember saying it. Part of your job is to remind this person of the statement after the interview and before the reference check.

A good quote can be picked up in your initial re-contact conversation before the interview. "Yes, I remember you; I think you were the most reliable worker I ever had." This can and should be worked into the interview if it can be done well. A little gentle prompting may be necessary with some. You might ask something like, "Did you consider me a good employee?" or "Would you consider me as one of your better workers?"

Let it be a two-way process. You could say things about how you enjoyed working with or for him or how you consider her the best boss you ever had. This is assuming that you truly consider the person as such.

Letters of Reference

Some employers will ask for letters of reference or recommendations from certain classes of people. This can include a professional in the field related to the job you are applying for or former supervisors. This presents a slightly different twist because some references do not know exactly what to say or do not have the time to write a letter.

Many will ask you to write the letter, and they will sign it. This is acceptable if you are certain that they agree with what is in the letter they are going to sign. With a former supervisor still at the same organization, try to get the letter done on organizational letterhead.

Most employers do not ask for letters of reference and will ignore them if submitted with a resume unsolicited. Many do not trust a letter that just says you worked some place and you were wonderful.

It is a common practice to give someone a letter of reference even if they were asked to resign or even fired. This is not ethical, but unfortunately it is commonplace and may have even been done at some point by the person you are now applying to.

It is a defense mechanism by the employer, who is hoping he will escape some of the hard feelings or even a lawsuit by the fired employee. You can then see why such unsolicited letters are often not helpful.

Example

An example of a typical short letter of recommendation is found on the next page.

The Greatkind Company
Attleworth, Colorado

July 4, 1976

To whom it may concern:

Miss Terri Smith worked for me as my executive secretary from June 12, 1970 until this date. She was an outstanding employee and made my job very much easier by her efforts. I would heartily recommend her to any job that she felt capable of.

Please feel free to call me at (123) 456-7899 for any questions that I may answer about Miss Smith's employment.

Sincerely.

Mary R. Bottenns
President

Section Four

Going Into Action

The Accelerated Job Search

Chapter

12

Cold Calling ....or Not

None But the Brave

As mentioned earlier, cold calling is not for everyone. When done correctly, it is highly effective; but when a job seeker is not the personality type to comfortably make cold calls, there can be a negative effect. If you have determined that there is no way that you can pick up a phone or knock on a door to contact strangers in your job search, then you may want to move on to the next chapter now. (See Chapter 1)

If you naturally make cold calls, have done so successfully either professionally or otherwise, or are just determined to try it in spite of your aversion, then read on. This method is highly proactive and expands the type of activities you will undertake considerably.

Where to Start

The first decision to make is whether to concentrate in very specific areas in which you have experience, training, and skills or to branch out into new and uncharted territory.

New areas can involve minor changes, such as related positions to what you have done or positions which would represent full blown career changes.

Speed Tip #23

Lay out specific positions and industries before you begin cold calling. Lack of focus here can cost valuable time.

Once you have made these decisions, you should map out the positions and industries you will target. If you are targeting a position which is generic to most industries, then you have a wide range of organizations.

These positions would include accounting, maintenance, human resources, training, clerical, and other jobs which are utilized across industry lines. Your own personal preferences both for and against certain industries can narrow the scope of the list.

A grid chart can be used to identify which combinations of position and industries you want to pursue. After some thought about qualifications and preferences, a grid chart can show at a glance the areas that you will be pursuing.

Look at the sample on the next page.

139

Industry	Positions			
	Clerical	Data Input	Reception	Billing
Legal	X			X
Insurance	X		X	X
Staffing	X		X	
Retail	X		X	
Education	X		X	
Food Svc.	X			
Medical		X		X
Manufact.	X		X	

The Contact List

After you determine the industries or types of organizations that you will be targeting, you need to build the list of those that you propose to contact. To do this, you will need to look at such resources as:

- Telephone yellow pages
- City directories
- Industry association rosters
- Chamber of commerce membership lists
- Internet searches
- Governmental organization directories

These and other sources will give the names, locations, and phone numbers of target organizations to contact. These will be organizations that contain the positions that you are pursuing. When you get your list completed, the next step is to prioritize the contacts.

Speed Tip #24

Prioritize your cold calling contact list by putting your best prospects at the top of your list.

Your best prospects will be in industries where you have experience and in organizations known to be hiring or expanding. Often you can tell who is hiring by scanning the help wanted ads for all positions.

If an organization is advertising for a lot of positions, it is an indication they may be expanding; and they may be looking for your type of position next. If they are on your list already, move them up in priority. If they are not on your list, give a second consideration to putting them there.

You can use a tracking chart to keep control of who you call and the results of the call. For each call you can use a call sheet. If you should happen to have a contact management computer program, it does all this for you. These programs will keep you organized and on track. Assuming here that you do not have such a program, let's take a look at a tracking sheet and a call sheet. This is used with call sheets and serves as a tool to keep your effort organized.

141

Tracking Sheet (not to scale)

Contact Name	Dates/Time Called	Next call
Company A		
Company B		
Organization C		
City D		

The Call Sheet

A call sheet is for a single contact and should have your "script" or opening statement on it as well as research details on the contact, specific results, information from the call, and next steps if any.

An example of one type is shown on the following page. Many forms work well; you must find what format works well for you.

Do not waste a lot of time trying to perfect it, but it must be good enough to be effective. Ensure that it is simple and comfortable for you.

CALL SHEET

Contact Name	Phone #
	Date/Time

Hi, this is John Brown calling; can you connect me to the person who does the hiring of engineers?

Talked to	Results:
Talked to	
Talked to	
Call other or later	Follow-up:

Arrange blank call sheets with contact only filled out in order of call priority. After you have made the call, arrange them with other documentation or information on the contact in order of your own categories. For follow-up, determine when you will call again and put the call sheet in the priority que on the tracking sheet for that future time and date.

Speed Tip #25
Stay Organized! Keep your call sheets and tracking sheets in priority order and you will avoid confusion and wasted time.

Cold Can Be Good

Cold calling may not be the most fun you ever had, but it can be highly effective, which can certainly lead to fun later on. If you are going to do it, do it well; and you will find that it will work for you.

Chapter

13

Networking

Warming to the Task

After a chapter about cold calling, a discussion of warm calling will round out the proactive calling area of your search. There are some that include cold calling within the scope of networking, but here we separate the types of calling between cold calling total strangers and calling someone with whom you already have a connection.

You will note that I did not say that networking should target only close friends; and I do not say that you need to target people you know, have worked with or even know casually.

You will be starting your networking with those that you have some *connection* to. A connection does not mean an existing relationship. It means that through a direct contact or through a series of connected contacts, you have a *path* to the individual you will be contacting.

These contacts can include:

- Current or former co-workers
- School and college instructors
- Relatives
- Business and residential neighbors
- Former customers or suppliers

146

- Religious associates
- Business association colleagues
- Friends and friends of friends

Obtaining a job through personal contact accounts for the highest percentage of success in job search. The percentage is usually quoted as somewhere above 60%. This is not always the result of an organized and structured effort, but it happens as a result of personal knowledge or contact.

It often happens when someone in a management meeting says: "We need to fill this position. Who do we know who would be a good candidate?" This means that they are looking for a known person. Possibly the person already works for the organization, does business with the organization, or is otherwise known to one or more managers in the organization.

Often these persons who are well known are approached about the job before they even know that there is a job opportunity in existence. They are made offers solely on their reputations with key persons in an organization.

Building your reputation with key individuals in your organization and in your industry can lead to your being approached for a position perhaps unknown to you. This is most effectively done over a long period while employed by the organization but can also be accomplished by contacting and staying in touch with key organizational and industry individuals. It is an effective process. What will be covered here is helping that process along.

Barriers

So what stops most people from networking? The answer is that the causes of inaction are some of the same as in cold calling strangers, but there are some different ones also. The barriers to starting a good network process can include:

- Awkwardness
- Embarrassment
- Self image problems
- Fear of failure

These are all natural feelings and are real barriers to getting the process started. Looking at them one by one and considering resolution may be helpful.

Awkwardness

Calling people may not be an activity you are comfortable with, and you feel that you will not come across well. You look to other activities that you are more comfortable with. You think that the other person will feel just as awkward as you will and that it would be a bad experience. Overcoming awkwardness can be accomplished by gaining familiarity with the process through practice. You can practice calling people other than your target individuals for other reasons. This bears no risk and will reduce the feeling of awkwardness.

Embarrassment

Feeling embarrassed about the situation of being in a job search is caused by a conception that your contacts will take pity on you, think poorly of you, or otherwise lower their opinions of you. This is rarely the case. Most often you will encounter a willingness to help. Most people spend at least some time in between positions at some point in their lives and can relate to your situation. You may be surprised to find that someone you call may also be involved in a job search.

Self Image Problems

Having worked for a time, most of us see ourselves as employed. The process of talking to others as an unemployed person alters that perception of ourselves. For some, this is understandably difficult. Looking at the process as the first part of

149

your next job can help overcome this problem. If you consider that you are moving through a normal and expected part of your career, much as nearly everyone does from time to time, you will realize that you are on track as you go through your job search.

Fear of Failure

A single battle is not the war. A number of actions will need to be performed before you start your next job. Probably none of them will lead immediately to your next job. It is all part of a process, and some actions will be more successful than others will.

Assuming that some minor failures are steps on the pathway to success, it is necessary that the process get started and that the varied results of your contacts are realized. (Remember that if you make 20 contacts, and only one is successful, it is not a 5% success. It is a 100% success.)

Jumping In

Getting started on a positive note is not a bad idea, so start your contacts with those people you know are your friends or who will undoubtedly give you a positive, helpful response. This gets you off to a running start, gives you a little practice, and builds confidence. Initial contacts should focus on the strength of the relationship while ensuring that you communicate that you are involved in a job search. You are not asking them for a job, just staying in touch, and asking if they might have information that could relate to possible job opportunities.

Advice on your job search is a valuable result of your contacts. It is usually freely given because of two reasons: It is flattering to be asked for advice, and it does not put the person under any pressure to come up with a job lead for you. This advice can be in many areas and may include:

- How to approach a certain expanding company.
- What some hiring managers are looking for.
- How to detect when a company may be expanding or hiring.
- Companies or organizations to stay away from.
- Referrals to valuable contacts.
- Information on corporate cultures.
- Associations to join.
- Meetings, conventions, and seminars to attend.
- Dress and grooming patterns of specific organizations.
- How to raise your profile among those who could be hiring.

This type of inside advice cannot be bought. Career counselors, job developers, recruiters, and consultants may have some of this advice; but if you get through to current up-to-date insiders, they will have the best advice by far. It is not only the best, but it is free.

Good advice will save you from wasted effort and wrong directions. It is to be sought at every opportunity during your job search. Not all the advice you get will be helpful, which will test your skills of quality discrimination. Most will be of value to your job search, and should be used in your planning and strategy.

Technique is All-Important

Planning what you will do in advance is preferable to picking up the phone and playing it by ear. Even if you are very comfortable making contact calls, it will pay for you to carefully plan what you are about to do.

The contacts you will call or meet with are limited and should be treated as any limited resource. They should be conserved, respected, and valued. Charging in without a plan and making poor use of your networking contacts is wasteful and defeating.

Each one should be analyzed separately and planned for separately.

Contact Analysis

In your survey of potential contacts, you should prioritize them in order of their value to your job search. A good order would be:

1. Persons who can actually hire you.
2. Persons who strongly influence someone who can hire you.
3. Persons who have specific information that can help you get hired.
4. Persons who have general information or knowledge which can assist in your job search.
5. People with positive attitudes who support you in your goals.

Starting with the highest priority contacts and focusing on your goal of getting a job. you will give greatest attention to these high priority contacts. Once you have identified who you will contact, you need to maximize your knowledge about the person in order to increase the quality of your approach.

Preparing for your call should include determination of the person's status and influence; things going on in their lives; things going on in their organization and industry, and any other personal or professional information that will affect how they can help you.

Next try to determine how your contact with these folks will be of benefit to them. If you cannot think of a way, consider these possibilities:

- The contact will be flattered.
- The contact feels good about helping someone.
- The contact knows that favors are often repaid.
- The contact enjoys counseling, coaching, and giving advice.

Knowing that you can give these benefits to the contact person cannot help but give you confidence by realizing the interchange is mutually beneficial. You are not asking for a one-way gift, you are entering into a synergy.

Calling

Making the call after all of your preparation puts you into an important phase of your search. Whether you are making the call in person or on the telephone, there are some important actions to keep in mind.

- **Attire**. Even if you are calling on the phone, dress at least to the level that your contact will be dressed. Never dress more casual. Your self-image is strongly affected by your dress. It comes across the phone line, and you will sound less confident. If you are sitting on the bed in your bedroom dressed in nightclothes or a sweatsuit and you know your contact that you are talking to is in business attire, you will be affected.

- **This is**. Your opening words should indicate that the contact knows you or should know you. Start with "This is Joe", not "My name is Joe".

- **Smile**. A smile or a frown can be "heard" over the telephone. Use your best smile.

- **Purpose**. After pleasantries, clearly state the purpose of your call. Do not hint, infer, insinuate or play games. Honesty and clarity are appreciated.

- **Advice**. When advice is given, make every effort to act on it if you feel it is worthwhile. Let the contact know you have followed the advice.

- **Thanks**. Always thank the contacts for whatever help you are given even if it is just for their time in listening to you.

155

Follow-up

Always follow up after making contact. This can be either verbally or in writing, but there is always a reason. At the very least a thank you and possibly an additional question or possibly to inform the contact that you have taken some of the advice that was given to you.

Staying in touch is usually very worthwhile. Sometimes a contact will come into new information but does not realize or remember that it could be of help to you. An additional call a few weeks later could be crucial in obtaining new information.

A good contact is a good contact even after you have obtained the job you want. A strong network is valuable and should be continued indefinitely. Perhaps you will be the helpful contact next time. In any case, stay with it and maintain your valuable asset.

Chapter

14

Responding to Advertised Postings

The Want Ads

The "Want Ads" are the most traditional and widely used single process to match job seekers with jobs. It is so widely used and has been for so long that it has become an icon for job search.

The picture of someone looking through the classified advertising section of a newspaper equates more with job search than all other possibilities combined. If you wanted to show a picture of someone in a job search that would relate to the most people, you would show an image of a person looking through the classified ads.

As old a method as it is, it still works to find a job. It should not be your only source of job leads, but that does not mean it should be downplayed.

Many good jobs are found in all forms of posted openings including newspaper ads, trade magazines, Internet websites, job flyers, telephone job hotlines, bulletin boards, and other postings.

A systematic search of these sources should be a part of your search plan. You will determine from your own experience how long it takes you to search each source, which in turn will allow you to plan your time more effectively.

Newspapers Classifieds – "Old Reliable"

Using the newspaper can be done by obtaining and searching the paper itself or by searching it online by computer. It's cheaper and faster to search by computer, but it is also easy to miss opportunities.

Classified ads are structured alphabetically by first word or category. This makes it very possible to miss what you are looking for if you either search on the computer by category key word or look in the paper in a particular area only.

What you are searching for may be listed under a word you were not expecting. For instance, if you are an engineer, the job could also be listed as a technician, specialist, or under an industry or type key word. This might appear as field engineer, regional engineer, product engineer, managing engineer, coordinating engineer, professional engineer, or one of many others.

Say you are a teacher or trainer. You might see what you are searching for under education, instruction, teachers, instructors, training, personnel, human resources, school, college, university, professional development, management development, or one of many others. If you are serious, you need to look at *every ad* to make sure you are not missing an opportunity. This is better done with the actual paper. Looking at out-of-area newspapers is probably better done by the computer.

Knowing certain "code words" can also help. Examples:

- Fast-paced = incredibly busy.
- Self-sufficient = very little support.
- Flexible = shaky & indecisive management.
- Management Trainee = expect overtime without pay.
- Recent graduates = over 30 need not apply.
- Mature attitude = older worker.
- Desired = strongly preferred.
- Preferred = mandatory.
- Salary depending on experience = we will try and lowball your salary.
- Continuous opening = we can't fill the positions.
- Excellent ethics, honesty, etc. = we just fired someone who didn't have these.
- Project = temporary job.
- No phone calls = we don't have a personnel department.

Reading every ad listed has several advantages, including:

- Catching ads that were incorrectly classified in the wrong area.
- Ads that were victims of misspelling.
- Ads listed in the wrong industry.
- You might find a job you were not looking for but that you are highly qualified for.

There are many ways of searching, depending on your personal preference and experience, but one method you might find helpful is as follows:

1. Read through once, using a highlighter, and highlight every ad that you even remotely could be interested in.
2. Review just the highlighted ads and cut out the best ones. (Be careful to check what is on the other side of the page when you cut.)
3. Carefully review just the ads you have cut out to select the final ones that you will respond to.

Speed Tip #26

Obtain newspapers from your most likely geographical target areas, but search secondary markets more quickly using on-line classified search websites such as careerpath.com.

Trade Magazines and Newsletters

Many trade journals and trade newsletters have sections for positions available in the industry on which they focus. As many of these publications are either regional or national in coverage, the position will most probably not be just down the block, but if you are willing to re-locate, they may be helpful.

Some of the magazines are carried in libraries, and the libraries carry directories which list the different journals. You can also find them at locations where organizations of the particular covered industry are located.

Going On Line

A number of types of Internet websites feature postings of available jobs. These include on-line newspaper classified ads; (both individual newspapers and sites featuring many newspapers' classified job postings); state employment agencies, government personnel offices; individual organization websites that have a jobs section; and numerous others. Exploring on the net you will discover many others.

Once you have found the sites that most closely fit your search, check them at least once a week.

Weekly is the most common update interval. If you do not have Internet access at home, you might try libraries, state employment services, or some quick print shops. They are good sources of Internet access.

Telephone Hot Lines

Many organizations have 24-hour job "hot lines" featuring recordings of available jobs that they are trying to fill. Most are updated weekly and include instructions on how to apply for their positions. You can build your own list quickly by calling the human resource departments of the organizations you feel you might be interested in working for. Many job seekers put the hot lines on speed dial and listen to the recordings on the telephone's speaker. Check each about once a week.

Flyers

Job announcement flyers generally give fairly complete information on the position, the hiring organization, closing dates, and the selection process. They can be found on bulletin boards, clipboards and in binders in personnel offices, job help centers, and in state employment offices. Most government personnel offices (city, county, state and federal) keep flyers from other government agencies and even some private organizations.

Whatever type of job postings you decide to make part of your job search plan, be sure to keep them organized and search them regularly.

Chapter

15

Battling Discrimination and Abuse

Still a Long Way to Go

Discrimination in hiring has been addressed at length by laws at all levels of government as well as new rules, regulations, policies, and protocols. Classes, seminars, and workshops have been held for hiring managers and human resource practitioners on avoiding discrimination both in hiring and on the job.

The good news from all this is that there truly has been an improvement in hiring practices to avoid much of the blatant discriminatory practices of the past. The bad news is that not only does discrimination still exist, but also *abuse* of applicants is very much in evidence and has not been seriously addressed by regulators or human resource professionals on a wide scale. We will look first at discrimination, then at abuse.

Discrimination Today

Despite the efforts made to eliminate it, many types of discrimination are practiced routinely throughout the working world. Among the most blatant and common are racial, gender, and age. Detecting or suspecting discrimination in individual cases is fairly easy compared to proving that it has happened, either consciously or unconsciously on the part of the hiring authority.

Proving cases of discrimination has been most successful when the ability to show patterns is present. When too few qualified applicants of a particular class are hired, this pattern can be used to implement corrective action. Several reasons can be the cause of discrimination.

- Blatant, fully intentional action on behalf of management to exclude specific classes of persons from being hired.
- Patterns of hiring which occur due to less-than-blatant acts but reflect feelings of discrimination.
- Problems in the hiring system which tend to exclude certain classes of people due to the way in which applicants are recruited, screened, interviewed, and selected.

Regardless of who you are, you can fall into a class of applicants which is discriminated against in some way by some hiring organization. You can be too young or too old, too tall or too short, too beautiful or too plain, too heavy or too thin, the wrong race, gender, religion, or nationality to please a given hiring manager.

You may discover blatant and illegal actions during the hiring process. A typical example of this would be illegal questions such as:

167

- Will you have any problems with childcare?
- Is there a chance your wife could be transferred?
- Will church attendance be a problem in your working Sundays?
- So where are you from originally?
- What year did you graduate from high school?
- Do you plan to have more children?
- Who did you vote for in the last election?
- Do you still live with your parents?

So Now What?

Once you have been confronted with an illegal and discriminatory act, such as being asked an inappropriate question, what are your options? They really boil down to two less-than-desirable choices:

1. Point out to the hiring manager that she cannot ask that question legally and that you refuse to answer it. You have done the right thing. You have defended your honor and your integrity. You have shown the organization how they might improve their hiring practices. Also, *you will not get the job.*
2. Swallow hard and briefly answer the question, then move the conversation quickly to another area.

If you choose door number one, you will not have the job; but you can file a complaint with the proper government authorities (like the EEOC) and help future applicants to avoid discrimination.

If you choose door number two, you may have a chance to win the job and at some point in the future fight against discrimination in that organization from the inside. If you do not get the job, you can still file the complaint. My advice is to take door number two.

Applicant Abuse – The Un-addressed Injustice

Unlike discrimination, regulators have not effectively addressed abuse of applicants. It is encountered so often it is expected and silently endured by applicants. Just because it is endured does not make it right, but your options when you encounter it are currently limited.

How are applicants abused? Let's look at what an applicant is. From the moment when a job seeker submits an application, a resume, or otherwise applies for a position, until formally notified of acceptance or rejection, the job seeker is an applicant. During this time, let us call it the Application Period, the applicant goes through a number of feelings while the hiring organization is going through the hiring process.

First we will look at what happens at a typical organization during a typical hiring process. Then we will look at what the applicant is going through during that same period.

ABC company decides it needs to replace a departed Systems Operator. The Systems Manager notifies the Personnel Manager, who starts the process. An ad is run in the local Sunday newspaper, and the job is posted on the ABC job hotline and the ABC website. The first resumes come in to Personnel and the Application Period has started.

The resumes are forwarded to the Systems Manager, who saves them in a file for a few days, then decides to review them after his return from a business trip, which takes a week. On his return work has piled up so he needs three days of catch-up before he can review the resumes. He then looks them over at high speed and goes with a personal "feel" to determine which of the 55 resumes he will select for an interview. He picks seven to proceed with. He notifies Personnel, which schedules the interviews on a Thursday morning in the following week by phoning the applicants. He also asks his assistant to sit in on the interviews.

The applicants come to the interview, and after all seven are finished, the Systems Manager discusses the applicants with his assistant and makes a choice of the top two applicants. Since important meetings are pressing, he notifies Personnel two days later to set up the two final interviews. Three days after that Personnel calls the final two candidates and schedules them in on a Monday afternoon.

At the final interview, two Systems Operators join the Systems Manager. These are long interviews. After a final selection is made, Personnel is asked to make reference checks, which takes 3 days to get through to all of them. The Systems Manager gets the results, which are good, so he then calls the chosen candidate and makes a job offer, which is accepted.

Post cards are sent a week later to the other six finalists, including the other candidate (in the final two) who was not selected, thanking them for their interest. The Application Period for those not selected has lasted approximately 8 weeks.

All those involved at ABC felt that the hiring went well and was somewhat routine. They were right about it being routine; but from the point of view of the applicants, it did not go well. None complained to ABC or to a regulatory agency. None filed a lawsuit. Not one applicant filed any type of protest. So how were they abused? What could ABC have done better?

We will discuss the answers to these questions after looking at an applicant's view.

A Silent Suffering

The typical applicant for a position of this type is not different from most other applicants. Let's follow Jack through his application with ABC. Jack has been unemployed for two months and has been through two interviews, neither of which resulted in employment.

He sees the ad in his Sunday paper for a position as a Systems Operator with ABC and decides to reply. Jack feels very good about his chances of success, because his qualifications appear to closely match or exceed what ABC was looking for. He sends his resume in on Monday with a cover letter and waits for a response.

While waiting, he talks with his family and friends regularly about his job search. He tells several people that he feels he may have a chance with ABC. After waiting a week and hearing nothing, Jack feels a bit concerned and calls ABC Personnel Department to see if they received his resume. A Personnel Clerk tells him that all the resumes received were forwarded to the Systems Manager. She has no separate list, so she tells him it "probably" arrived but cannot confirm

172

it. Jack now gets frustrated and a bit upset, because he does not know what the status is on this possible future career. Does he send in a duplicate resume? He decides not to.

After waiting two weeks, Jack feels that the chances are very slim he will hear anything from ABC and essentially writes off the prospect. He feels bad and cannot understand why he was rejected.

After three weeks, he is surprised to hear from a Personnel Clerk at ABC who is scheduling interviews for the following week with the Systems Manager. Jack's emotions take another turn as he again adjusts to the possibility of employment at ABC.

He prepares for the interview. He tells family and friends that he has a promising interview coming up, explaining that this was the opportunity that he had written off.

Jack goes to the interview and feels good about how it went. His background is a very good fit for the job, he thinks. Now he again waits with no information about what is going on at ABC, but he has no reason to believe it is not the final interview. He expects some kind of notification in a day or two of the final selection – either a job offer or a rejection. Waiting at this point is agonizing. His wife and family wait with him, wondering what is going on. After two days, he again starts to assume that no news is bad news. But why can't they at least tell him he has not been selected?

Jack is starting to have feelings of frustration and anger at ABC for inflicting pain on him by keeping him in the dark. When, at five days, Personnel at ABC calls and wants to schedule another interview; he feels surprise, stress, some optimism, and some suspicion. Why was he not told at the first interview that there may be another interview? How many candidates are still in the running? Five? One? What can he do to prepare for the second interview? What is the purpose of this interview and who will be there? Not knowing what is happening is causing Jack to lose sleep, and he gets cranky and irritable.

The second interview is held and Jack feels he has done very well. The interviewers praised him and talked about how well he would fit in. He is now feeling optimistic again but still resentful of not being told what was happening. This time he asks the interviewers when they might make a decision. They tell him "soon".

He tells himself not to get stressed waiting, but that is not possible. He is confident but starts the same wait one more time with its accompanying agony. He thinks about how it will be working at ABC, but his wife reminds him he has not yet been offered the job. A week of waiting now causes unbelievable worry, stress, and frustration. His feelings toward ABC now are very mixed.

At last Jack receives a rejection postcard from Personnel thanking him for his interest and time. He is of course devastated, confused, and highly resentful.

Is There an Evil Empire?

Having looked at what happened on both sides of an all-too-typical hiring process, what should you understand as a job seeker facing organizations that are conducting hiring processes? A few points:

- The torture inflicted upon you is not done on purpose. It is caused by a hiring team who are both totally focused on getting someone hired and not trained on how to conduct an applicant-friendly process. They abuse you without realizing it.
- Fighting the system will not help you get hired.
- Ask questions about what the process will be at each step. This will often help, but hiring managers do not always stick to what they tell you they intend to do. Their focus is on their own needs, not yours.

175

- Remember that there is no good way to know what is going on without getting overly "pushy" and jeopardizing your chances.

- When you get hired and become the hiring manager, keep your applicants totally informed of the process at every step. Do not pass the abuse along.

Being abused during the Application Period is not fun, and it is not right; but it is unfortunately the reality we face today. Fight it when you can, and do not commit it when you are hiring.

Chapter

16

Creating a Job

As If By Magic

Creating a job for yourself where none existed before is the most proactive form of job search. However it is accomplished, it takes some different skills than those needed in the search for an existing job. It also shares the need for certain skills and personal assets such as perseverance, positive attitude, belief in yourself, and some skills in persuasion.

We will look at five of the most common ways to create jobs and some aspects of each method. These five are:

- Become a consultant.
- Become a contract employee.
- Start or buy a company.
- Point out the need, same organization.
- Point out the need from outside.

Becoming a Consultant

Your education, experience, skills, and abilities are valuable to some organizations who are willing to pay for your short term services to improve or assist their operations. You can contract with them on a special arrangement to assist them with a particular situation. In order for this to happen, the following things must occur:

178

- A need must exist.
- The organization with the need must recognize the need.
- The organization must want a consultant to address the need.
- The consultant must discover the need and make contact with the organization.
- The organization must become convinced that the consultant can and should help it.
- Both parties must agree on terms and compensation.

Consulting often looks very inviting to those who have not tried it. They see freedom, prestige, high levels of compensation, choice of assignments, and liberal time off as the key points of the consulting method of work. It sounds glamorous and romantic; dashing about the country; admired as an expert; listened to by the heads of business.

The truth about consulting is that it is not glamorous but usually very hard work. The assignments are not always the ones you want; and the majority of your time is spent on marketing, writing proposals, and otherwise trying to land an assignment. The high hourly rates are for short periods. The compensation for marketing and proposing is zero. Frustration and stress levels are often high for consultants and turnover is brisk. It takes months or even years to build any kind of client base.

Some consultants do well, in spite of the odds, and enjoy this type of work. It covers all industries and career fields and can be short term, long term, renewable, contingent, hourly, or flat fee. Often consultants are paid for their knowledge rather than their hard work, but not always. The old joke about this is as follows:

It seems that Wally, the chief engineer of the power plant at a remote little town, announced that he was about to retire and suggested to the powers that be that he needed to train a replacement. Management ignored his suggestion; and felt that since they had never had real problems with the aging plant, they could hire a new graduate engineer in due course. They were not worried.

Wally indeed retired. About two weeks after the retirement, a brand new college graduate engineer was hired. A week after that the plant stopped working at 1 AM in the morning. The new engineer was called, and after two hours of trying to find the problem, he admitted he was stumped.

Management called Wally, who lived nearby, and asked if he could help. He informed them that his fee would be $10,000. Finding this unacceptable, management offered 1½ times his old hourly rate with a two-hour minimum. Wally laughed. The new engineer then tried again and failed. It was now 4 AM, and the town was still without power. Management called Wally back and agreed to his terms.

Wally went to the plant in his old overalls, crawled way back among the pipes, looked around for a minute, then banged on one particular pipe with his hammer. The plant immediately fired up and was back in operation.

Management received the bill from Wally: $10,005. They asked Wally why the odd amount. He answered: "Five dollars for banging on the pipe. Ten thousand for knowing where to bang." Consultants have unique knowledge.

Becoming a Contract Employee

Contract employment is similar to regular employment except that you are the employee of a contractor and do the actual work at the contractor's client company. It is also called agency work, employee leasing, and other names. You can sign up with a contract company and wait for an assignment or respond to calls for contract employees which appear in many of the same places that ordinary jobs are posted. Contracting can be to your benefit if the job disappears, because the contractor or agency may be able to place you in another contract position.

Starting or Buying a Company

The apparent glamour of running your own business and/or being your own boss should not be the reason you choose this option. Most businesses fail. Failing is not glamorous. If you know what you are doing, have been in the business before, and are well financed, this could be a possibility. If, however, you are an accountant and want to jump into the restaurant business, or you are a landscaper and want to be the new shoe king of your city, I would recommend a long look before leaping.

Running a small business is hard work, stressful, and requires many specific skills to succeed. Bookkeeping, marketing, budgeting, and many other tasks must be done correctly. If you buy a franchise, help is often available from the franchiser on these key skills. Local community colleges also have business courses which can be of assistance.

Going into business should not be a lightly regarded decision. If you hire others, their futures, as well as your own, are then dependent on your business capabilities. Anyone investing in your business is also depending on your success. The most successful businesses are well financed and have operators who know the business end as well as the specific industry part of the operation.

Pointing Out the Need in the Same Company

If you are currently employed, there may be an opportunity to point out the need for a specific new position which has not previously existed. If you can get to the decision maker on such things and convince this party of two things, you may have a chance at a bigger and better job. The two things:

1. Why the organization needs this particular new position, and
2. Why the ideal person for the new job is you.

Such things as a better organization; adding to the bottom line financially; saving money or time; improving the organizational image; or other solid benefits may help you make your point as to need. Selling yourself will depend partly on your performance history in your current position.

Pointing Out the Need from Outside

A more difficult proposition, but still possible, is to convince the management of a strange company, which does not currently employ you, of the same two things as you would internally. Here you need to know the business well and have information or an idea that they do not have. A new product that you can help develop is an example.

Not for the Weak-Hearted

Creating a job is for assertive individuals. If you are a follower or are very adverse to risk, you are probably better advised to pursue an existing job. But if you are adventurous, creative, and highly self-confident, job creation might be your ticket.

Section Five

Contact

The Accelerated Job Search

Chapter

17

Interviewing Concepts

Meeting Your Future

Entering the interview room and meeting your interviewer(s) can be the equivalent of meeting your future. If you do well, these could be your future co-workers. If it does not go as well as you might have wished, another opportunity elsewhere is waiting.

The time spent in an interview is a very important part of determining your working future. Preparation for it is therefore critical to your future success.   There are specific *always* and *never* suggestions I would give you. They are as follows:

Always

- **Always** arrive early, at least 5 – 10 minutes, but no more than 15.   You do not want to make the interviewer feel rushed, and you do not want to appear that you had the time wrong.
- **Always** bring a copy of any resume , cover letter, application, or job description with you for reference. Occasionally interviewers will, for some reason, not have your information in front of them. This happens more often than you might think. Having a copy with you can help the process.
- **Always** research the organization to find out what you can about it prior to the interview. You can do this at your library, the Internet, or through other

resources such as employees or organizational annual reports.

- **Always** prepare a short list of questions to ask the interviewer. These can be used to get information you want or need, to show interest, to respond to the question: "Do you have any questions for me?", and to divert the course of questioning should it go into an area you are less than comfortable with.

- **Always** be extremely courteous to every person you meet from the time you enter the building. Play it safe and assume every person will talk to the interviewer or is involved somehow in the hiring process.

- **Always** think of the interviewer as a person you like very much. Think about this even before you meet the person or persons. After all, they are giving you a chance at this job, right? When you do this, it will show in your demeanor, and you will appear more positive.

- **Always** review a list of most often asked questions on interviews, practice, and be sure of your answers. See the list in this book. This will assist you in appearing more poised and confident.

- **Always** maintain a positive attitude seeing yourself in the position. You are being assessed as a possible member of the team. Help the interviewer visualize you as a team member who gets along and fits in. A positive attitude supports this.

189

- **Always** smile and maintain good eye contact with the interviewer. This keeps a positive feeling going and avoids any perception of negative or deceptive intent on your part.

- **Always** use a firm handshake. This shows confidence and a good attitude.

- **Always** check your appearance just before the interview. A lot can happen between your initial dressing/grooming and your arrival at the interview site.

- **Always** try to discuss your accomplishments that relate to the position for which you have applied. Other great deeds may be impressive, and you may enjoy telling about them; but unless they in some way relate to the position being discussed, they are only a distraction.

- **Always** ask what the next step in the hiring process is if the interviewer has not told you. This not only shows your confidence that you have done well but gets the interviewer to think of you as still being a player as the process moves forward.

- **Always** try to get a business card from the interviewer so that you may write and correctly address a thank you letter. If you are not able to do this during the interview, ask the receptionist or other employee on the way out for the correct information. Most often they will assist you.

Never

- **Never** wear high fashion or loud colored clothing or jewelry to an interview. Avoid anything that is not conservative in nature. Wait until after you are hired to display your contemporary fashion tastes.
- **Never** smoke or be around cigarette smoke for two hours before the interview. The smoke is easy to smell and may negatively impress a non-smoking interviewer. The same may be said for very heavy perfume or cologne.
- **Never** bring anyone with you to an interview. If someone provided transportation, have the person wait someplace other than the waiting room or immediate area of the interview.
- **Never** bring a briefcase with you unless necessary to carry work samples. If carrying a purse, make it a small one. A letter sized binder or portfolio in a dark color is fine. Remember you are carrying copies of your resume, cover letter, and/or application, as well as a list of references, in case you are asked.
- **Never** drink a lot of fluid right before the interview. It is awkward to ask to use the restroom during an interview.
- **Never** wear association or other pins unless related to the position. It is distracting, and may appear as an attempt at one-upmanship.

- **Never** accept coffee or other drink unless the interviewer is also having refreshment. It is only a distraction and you may spill it, rattle the cup, or commit another awkward moment. It happens.

- **Never** give a salary amount. If asked, ask the interviewer what the range is and respond to that.

- **Never** ask what the pay is during the interview. If an offer is made, the pay being offered will be stated at that point. You may negotiate after the offer.

- **Never** lower your eyes when you are asked a question – it makes you look guilty and negative.

- **Never** lie or give a false impression. Assume you will be discovered.

- **Never** speak badly of a former boss, co-worker, or organization. Doing so displays disloyalty and projects that behavior into possible future jobs.

- **Never** chew gum during the interview.

- **Never** comment on items in the interviewer's office. This can be dangerous because you do not know how the interviewer feels about the items. Even harmless comments can backfire.

- **Never** discuss family, religion, or politics. These are areas the interviewer is not allowed by law to get into. Do not give up this protection. They are not safe areas.

- **Never** assume you are not doing well and give up on the interview. Some interviewers intentionally

192

conduct the interview in such a way as to make you think you are not doing well. Keep smiling no matter what.

- **Never** sit down until asked to do so by the interviewer, either by word or gesture. It may appear presumptive.

Interviewing Preparation Assistance

Preparation for an interview is often much more effective if you have assistance. The following people may be your best help in preparing:

- An experienced interviewer who will give you a tough practice interview. If you can videotape this practice for your later review, you will find it of immense assistance. (See Chapter 21)
- A close associate who will, from time to time in conversation, ask you a difficult interview question when you are off-guard to sharpen your quick thinking.
- A grooming expert to advise you on clothing, hair, makeup, etc. (See Chapter 23)
- Your family and friends who best know your communications strengths and weaknesses and can help you minimize problems while utilizing your strengths.
- An industry expert who can update you on the latest industry concerns and hot topics. You can

193

use this information to show you are current in industry topics.

- An employee of the target company can assist in getting you up to speed on inside organizational concerns.

No period of time may be more important to your professional life than the interview. Do not spare the effort in your preparation.

Chapter

18

50 Frequently Asked Questions

Interview Question Strategy

Review these typical interview questions and think about how you would answer them. Many of them have numerous versions. After your initial review, look at the same list with the strategy suggestions and comments.

1. Tell me about yourself.
2. Why did you leave your last job?
3. What experience do you have in this field?
4. Do you consider yourself successful?
5. What do co-workers say about you?
6. What do you know about this organization?
7. What have you done to improve your knowledge in the last year?
8. Are you applying for other jobs?
9. Why do you want to work for this organization?
10. Do you know anyone who works for us?
11. What kind of salary do you need?
12. Are you a team player?
13. How long would you expect to work for us if hired?
14. Have you ever had to fire anyone? How did you feel about that?
15. What is your philosophy towards work?
16. If you had enough money to retire right now, would you?
17. Have you ever been asked to leave a position?

18. Explain how you would be an asset to this organization.
19. Why should we hire you?
20. Tell me about a suggestion you have made.
21. What irritates you about co-workers?
22. What is your greatest strength?
23. Tell me about your dream job.
24. Why do you think you would do well at this job?
25. What are you looking for in a job?
26. What kind of person would you refuse to work with?
27. What is more important to you: the money or the work?
28. What would your previous supervisor say your strongest point is?
29. Tell me about a problem you had with a supervisor.
30. What has disappointed you about a job?
31. Tell me about your ability to work under pressure.
32. Do your skills match this job or another job more closely?
33. What motivates you to do your best on the job?
34. Are you willing to work overtime? Nights? Weekends?
35. How would you know you were successful on this job?
36. Would you be willing to relocate if required?
37. Are you willing to put the interests of the organization ahead of your own?
38. Describe your management style.

39. What have you learned from mistakes on the job?
40. Do you have any blind spots?
41. If you were hiring a person for this job, what would you look for?
42. Do you think you are overqualified for this position?
43. How do you propose to compensate for your lack of experience?
44. What qualities do you look for in a boss?
45. Tell me about a time when you helped resolve a dispute between others.
46. What position do you prefer on a team working on a project?
47. Describe your work ethic.
48. What has been your biggest professional disappointment?
49. Tell me about the most fun you have had on the job.
50. Do you have any questions for me?

Now Let's Talk Strategy

Now review the list again and consider some strategy suggestions and comments. Remember to consider different versions.

1. Tell me about yourself.
The most often asked question in interviews. You need to have a short statement prepared in your mind.

Be careful that it does not sound rehearsed. Limit it to work-related items unless instructed otherwise. Talk about things you have done and jobs you have held that relate to the position you are interviewing for. Start with the item farthest back and work up to the present.

2. Why did you leave your last job?
Stay positive regardless of the circumstances. Never refer to a major problem with management and never speak ill of supervisors, co-workers, or the organization.

If you do, you will be the one looking bad. Keep smiling and talk about leaving for a positive reason such as an opportunity, a chance to do something special, or other forward-looking reasons.

3. What experience do you have in this field?
Speak about specifics that relate to the position you are applying for. If you do not have specific experience, get as close as you can.

4. Do you consider yourself successful?
You should always answer yes and briefly explain why. A good explanation is that you have set goals, and you have met some and are on track to achieve the others.

5. What do co-workers say about you?

Be prepared with a quote or two from co-workers. Either a specific statement or a paraphrase will work. "Jill Clark, a co-worker at Smith Company, always said I was the hardest worker she had ever known." It is as powerful as Jill having said it at the interview herself.

6. What do you know about this organization?

This question is one reason to do some research on the organization before the interview. Find out where they have been, and where they are going. What are the current issues, and who are the major players?

7. What have you done to improve your knowledge in the last year?

Try to include improvement activities that relate to the job. A wide variety of activities can be mentioned as positive self-improvement. Have some good ones handy to mention.

8. Are you applying for other jobs?

Be honest but do not spend a lot of time in this area. Keep the focus on this job and what you can do for this organization. Anything else is a distraction.

9. Why do you want to work for this organization?

This may take some thought and certainly should be based on the research you have done on the organization. Sincerity is extremely important here, and will easily be sensed. Relate it to your long-term career goals.

10. Do you know anyone who works for us?

Be aware of the policy on relatives working for the organization. This can affect your answer even though they asked about friends not relatives. Be careful to mention a friend only if they are well thought of.

11. What kind of salary do you need?

A loaded question. A nasty little game that you will probably lose if you answer first. So, do not answer it. Instead, say something like: "That's a tough question. Can you tell me the range for this position?" In most cases, the interviewer, taken off guard, will tell you. If not, say that it can depend on the details of the job. Then give a wide range.

12. Are you a team player?

You are, of course, a team player. Be sure to have examples ready. Specifics that show you often perform for the good of the team rather than for yourself are good evidence of your team attitude. Do not brag, just say it in a matter-of-fact tone. This is a key point.

13. How long would you expect to work for us if hired?

Specifics here are not good. Something like this should work: "I'd like it to be a long time." or "As long as we both feel I'm doing a good job."

14. Have you ever had to fire anyone? How did you feel about that?

This is serious. Do not make light of it or in any way seem like you like to fire people. At the same time, you will do it when it is the right thing to do. When it comes to the organization versus the individual who has created a harmful situation, you will protect the organization. Remember firing is not the same as layoff or reduction in force.

15. What is your philosophy towards work?

The interviewer is not looking for a long or flowery dissertation here. Do you have strong feelings that the job gets done? Yes. That's the type of answer that works best here. Short and positive, showing a benefit to the organization.

16. If you had enough money to retire right now, would you?

Answer yes if you would. But since you need to work, this is the type of work you prefer. Do not say yes if you do not mean it.

202

17. Have you ever been asked to leave a position?

If you have not, say no. If you have, be honest, brief, and avoid saying negative things about the people or organization involved.

18. Explain how you would be an asset to this organization.

You should be anxious for this question. It gives you a chance to highlight your best points as they relate to the position being discussed. Give a little advance thought to this relationship.

19. Why should we hire you?

Point out how your assets meet what the organization needs. Do not mention any other candidates to make a comparison.

20. Tell me about a suggestion you have made.

Have a good one ready. Be sure and use a suggestion that was accepted and was then considered successful. One related to the type of work applied for is a real plus.

21. What irritates you about co-workers?

This is a trap question. Think "real hard" but fail to come up with anything that irritates you. A short statement that you seem to get along with folks is great.

22. What is your greatest strength?
Numerous answers are good, just stay positive. A few good examples:

- Your ability to prioritize.
- Your problem-solving skills.
- Your ability to work under pressure.
- Your ability to focus on projects.
- Your professional expertise.
- Your leadership skills.
- Your positive attitude.

23. Tell me about your dream job.
Stay away from a specific job. You cannot win. If you say the job you are contending for is it, you strain credibility. If you say another job is it, you plant the suspicion that you will be dissatisfied with this position if hired. The best bet is to stay generic and say something like: "A job where I love the work, like the people, can contribute, and can't wait to get to work."

24. Why do you think you would do well at this job?
Give several reasons and include skills, experience, and interest.

25. What are you looking for in a job?
See answer #23.

26. What kind of person would you refuse to work with?

Do not be trivial. It would take disloyalty to the organization, violence or lawbreaking to get you to object. Minor objections will label you as a whiner.

27. What is more important to you: the money or the work?

Money is always important, but the work is the most important. There is no better answer.

28. What would your previous supervisor say your strongest point is?

There are numerous good possibilities:

- Loyalty
- Energy
- Positive attitude
- Leadership
- Team player
- Expertise
- Initiative
- Patience
- Hard Work
- Creativity
- Problem solver

29. Tell me about a problem you had with a supervisor.

Biggest trap of all. This is a test to see if you will speak ill of your boss. If you fall for it and tell about a problem with a former boss, you may well blow the interview right there. Stay positive and develop a poor memory about any trouble with a superior.

30. What has disappointed you about a job?

Safe areas are few but can include:

- Not enough of a challenge.
- You were laid off in a reduction.
- Company did not win a contract which would have given you more responsibility.

Don't get trivial or negative.

31. Tell me about your ability to work under pressure.

You may say that you thrive under certain types of pressure. Give an example that relates to the type of position applied for.

32. Do your skills match this job or another job more closely?

Probably this one. Do not give fuel to the suspicion that you may want another job more than this one.

33. What motivates you to do your best on the job?

This is a personal trait that only you can say, but good examples are:

- A challenge
- Achievement
- Recognition

34. Are you willing to work overtime? Nights? Weekends?

This is up to you. Be totally honest.

35. How would you know you were successful on this job?

Several ways are good measures:

- You set high standards for yourself and meet them.
- Your outcomes are a success.
- Your boss tells you that you are successful.

36. Would you be willing to relocate if required?

You should be clear on this with your family prior to the interview if you think there is a chance it may come up. Do not say yes just to get the job if the real answer is no. This can create a lot of problems later on in your career. Be honest at this point and save yourself future grief.

37. Are you willing to put the interests of the organization ahead of your own?

This is a straight loyalty and dedication question. Do not worry about the deep ethical and philosophical implications. Just say yes.

38. Describe your management style.

Try to avoid labels. Some of the more common labels, like "progressive", "salesman" or "consensus", can have several meanings or descriptions depending on which management expert you listen to. The "situational" style is safe, because it says you will manage according to the situation, instead of "one size fits all".

39. What have you learned from mistakes on the job?

Here you have to come up with something or you strain credibility. Make it a small, well-intentioned mistake with a positive lesson learned. An example would be: working too far ahead of colleagues on a project and thus throwing coordination off.

40. Do you have any blind spots?

Trick question. If you know about blind spots, they are no longer blind spots. Do not reveal any personal areas of concern here. Let them do their own discovery on your bad points. Do not hand it to them.

41. If you were hiring a person for this job, what would you look for?

Be careful to mention traits that are needed and that you have.

42. Do you think you are overqualified for this position?

Regardless of your qualifications, state that you are *very well* qualified for the position.

43. How do you propose to compensate for your lack of experience?

First, if you have experience that the interviewer does not know about, bring that up. Then, point out (if true) that you are a hard working quick learner.

44. What qualities do you look for in a boss?

Be generic and positive. Safe qualities are knowledgeable, a sense of humor, fair, loyal to subordinates, and holder of high standards. All bosses think they have these traits.

45. Tell me about a time when you helped resolve a dispute between others.

Pick a specific incident. Concentrate on your problem solving technique and not the dispute you settled.

46. What position do you prefer on a team working on a project?

Be honest. If you are comfortable in different roles, point that out.

47. Describe your work ethic.

Emphasize benefits to the organization. Things like "determination to get the job done" and "work hard but enjoy your work" are good.

48. What has been your biggest professional disappointment?

Be sure that you refer to something that was beyond your control. Show acceptance and no negative feelings.

49. Tell me about the most fun you have had on the job.

Talk about having fun by accomplishing something for the organization.

50. Do you have any questions for me?

Always have some questions prepared. Questions involving areas where you will be an asset to the organization are good. "How soon will I be able to be productive?" and "What type of projects will I be able to assist on?" are examples.

Chapter

19

Tough Stuff

Handling Tough Stuff

Many job seekers have barriers to employment that seem insurmountable in their quest for a good job. You may have problem areas in your history that would seem to eliminate you from the type of employment you would most like to secure.

These problems can include being fired or asked to resign; arrests and/or conviction for a crime; substance abuse problems; large gaps in employment; or other situations which may cause concerns to an employer.

Many people with these problems assume that they are hopelessly banned from decent employment for life. They feel that they are blacklisted from nearly all positions due to the perceptions by the employer that they will not fit or will cause problems. Some have found this to be true, having been rejected or eliminated from consideration for jobs for which they have applied.

There is no escaping the fact that some employers are unyielding in their opposition to hiring those with unfortunate situations in their history. What you will find, however, are many employers who are willing to give you a chance. This is due to many factors, not the least of which is that the hiring manager or family or friends have also had problems in their lives and can relate to your situation. Many who have recovered from problems feel that they now need to help others.

The important thing to remember if you have one of these problems is to remain positive and believe in yourself. If you strongly believe that you will be an asset to the hiring organization, that will come across in the interview. Maintain good eye contact and display confidence in your abilities. In no way should you be defensive, intimidated, or apologetic.

If the subject of a problem comes up, answer it honestly and very briefly; then get off the subject. The best way to move off a subject is to ask a question. Go to the interview armed with some good questions to ask and be prepared to use them. (See Chapter 20)

The Logic of Truth

We hear too often of lying in job interviews. (Reference the Management Advantage book: *"How to Spot a Liar in a Job Interview"* by this author.) Lying is always a bad idea. It keeps you from feeling good about yourself and adds to the tension you feel in the interview. You have to worry about how your lies match up, and the danger of looking foolish when a lie is brought to light.

213

Many interviewers are quite good at spotting untruths (especially those who have read my book, above) and will react with a totally negative response. Even if you are not detected lying in the interview, chances are excellent that you may be discovered in the future.

You are, therefore, waiting for that "tap on the shoulder" by the employer who has found out the truth and will then fire you for untruthfulness. All moral considerations aside, it just makes no sense to lie your way into a job and then wait for someone to find out the truth.

Truth is a wonderful thing. It is a stress reducer. It simplifies how you discuss your personal history. Since there is only one version of it, it is easier to remember than something made up.

Suggested Answers

In the chart that follows, you can see some suggestions for answering tough questions not only in the interview but for applications as well. These are only suggestions, but you can see how positive answers can be applied to almost any situation. Study them carefully.

214

Sample Answers to Tough Questions

Question	Possible Answer
Explain gaps in employment	Went to school
	Cared for children or elders
	Temporary medical problem
	Performed as a volunteer
	Self-employed
	Extended religious retreat
	Supported by spouse
	Other obligations
Why did you leave your last job?	Any of the above
	To pursue another opportunity
	Personal reasons
	Laid off due to no work, downsizing, etc.
Have you ever been arrested?	Yes, but not convicted
	Yes – an embarrassing situation - will explain details.
	Yes, but record has been cleared
	Yes, but charges were dismissed.
Have you ever been convicted of a crime?	I have no *record* of criminal conviction.
	Yes, but conviction is being cleared
	Yes, I welcome the opportunity to explain the circumstances.
Have you ever been fired or asked to resign from any job?	Yes, due to new management, internal politics, company reorg., or was whistleblower.
	Yes, after stating intent to resign.
	Yes - arranged circumstances.
Have you failed a pre-empl. or random drug screen?	Yes, and I have completed a treatment program.
	Yes, will explain unusual circumstances.

Emphasizing the positive and believing in yourself is the key rather than the answers themselves. You can do what you set out to do only if *you* believe it will happen.

Chapter

20

Questions to Ask

Sample Questions to Ask

Entering the interview room with some questions to ask the interviewer is an absolute must if you want to be properly prepared for a good interview. Interviewers often ask if you have questions for them. It shows you have some interest in the job and have given some thought to it.

Questions may be used to get away from subjects that you feel are not helping your cause. They also help you understand key points that may help you in answering other questions and deciding whether this is a job you want.

The following is a list of questions that you may choose from to ask during a job interview. The questions asked will vary according to each interview.

❑ Why is the job open/available?

The answer to this can be very valuable to you in shaping your answers to questions. If the previous person was fired for not being a team player, then you know to emphasize your team enhancing assets. You may also pick up other clues on what is desired for the position at the same time.

❑ What is the biggest challenge I would face on this job?

This gives you a chance to match your strengths against the dragon and show how you would be of most benefit to the organization. It may also give you information on priorities.

❑ What are this organization's short and long term goals?

Here you can show that you wish to contribute to the success of the organization.

❑ Six months from now, how will my success on the job be measured?

You are demonstrating that you expect to exhibit superior performance and expect that you will be held accountable.

❑ Who would by my immediate supervisor?

If you do not already know, you may find out that it is the interviewer who is to be your boss. It is in any case good information to know.

❑ What are the most important skills needed for this job?

This is an opportunity to point out a skill match or to do a crash course on a specific skill before you start, if you are hired.

❑ With whom would I be working, and what do they do?

You will get a better picture of the work dynamics from the answer to this question.

❑ How would you describe the ideal person for this position?

From this you can shape your image to fit the ideal as much as possible. Then again, if the ideal does not sound like you, maybe you do not want the job.

❑ Is overtime available or expected?

You are getting into the "long hours and hard work" part of the job, which is positive. Your are demonstrating that you are a hard worker and will do what it takes to complete the job.

❑ What is the career path for this position?

This shows you are interested in long term employment and will be doing your best work. Be careful if you are talking to your potential future boss, and your only upward step is her job.

❑ Is there training on the job?

You want to demonstrate that you like to stay up to date on your job and to learn new things. This question accomplishes that.

❑ Are there opportunities to cross-train?

A cross-trained employee is a more valuable employee, because it increases a supervisor's flexibility in assignments.

❑ Is this position expected to be permanent, long term?

This not only shows an interest in strategic employment, but lets you know if the job is expected to last. The job could be terrific but be slated to go away in six months. This kind of information could dissuade you from wanting the job.

❑ What kind of self-improvement is expected?

You are showing that you want to improve yourself and improve your work performance. This is a positive signal.

❑ Is there a mentoring program?

This is information for you to consider if this is a job with a steep learning curve. A mentor can be a tremendous assistance to you.

❑ What would be a typical day for the person in this job?

Here you are thinking yourself into the job, which shows confidence. Confidence can be contagious. The interviewer may catch it.

Chapter

21

Practice

Does Practice Make Perfect?

The old saying that "Practice Makes Perfect" is actually not true. Only *perfect* practice makes perfect. Practicing the wrong way will never allow you to improve. You will only learn very well how to do it wrong. Before setting out to practice your interviewing skills, go over Chapters 17, 18, 19, and 20. Then set up your interview practice plans.

A practice interview with an experienced interviewer is very helpful as you will get used to the interview setting and be more relaxed in the actual interview. If you can videotape a practice interview and review it, then practice again, you can iron out any problems you may see on the tape.

Practicing with someone as the interviewer, who is not experienced as such, can also be helpful, because many interviewers you may encounter are inexperienced also. Here you can practice guiding the interview into areas that exhibit your strong points. Inexperienced interviewers tend to talk too much and fail to control the interview to the point that they will never determine the critical facts they need for an informed decision.

Practice sessions with you acting as the interviewer tend to strengthen your self-confidence and de-mystify the process for you. You can feel what the interviewer is going through, and thereby better judge what their reactions might mean as you observe them observe you.

Practice in answering specific questions is a good way to prepare. You can take the 50 questions in Chapter 18 and have a friend or family member ask you versions of them out of order. This is a great activity for a car trip or a quiet time at home. If you do not have such help, you could record the questions on a small recorder and play them back one at a time, stopping the machine and answering them with your best unrehearsed responses.

If possible, try to duplicate the type of room and time of day most likely for your interview. This would most typically be a business office and in the morning or afternoon. Interviews are rarely in the evening. Make the practice sessions as realistic as possible, dressing for the part with business attire of the type that you plan to wear to the actual interview.

The Game

Both parties conduct the interview part of the selection process much like a game, with a game plan, strategy and tactics, scoring, maneuvering, positioning, regrouping, and finally winning or losing. Being

225

passed to the next level of the selection process signifies winning for you, while winning for the interviewer is selecting the best candidate for the position. No one knows all that they need or would like to know, so both parties operate with partial information.

Like you would do for a sporting game, you need to prepare in both mental and physical ways. A good diet and plenty of exercise will aid you in getting in shape for the game of interviewing. Your mental alertness is strongly influenced by your physical condition. (See Chapter 7) You will endanger your chances of having a good interview if you ignore this area.

Chapter

22

Phone Interviews

Just a Couple of Questions

You have applied for a number of jobs you spotted in the classified ads, on the Internet, and from referrals. You sent in resumes and cover letters and waited for the responses. The phone rings and a voice says: "This is Mr. Jones from XYZ Company. We received your resume, and I have a couple of questions if you have a moment."

Having applied for a number of jobs, you may first have to determine which company and which job Mr. Jones is calling about. You then must bring into your current focus what you stated on your resume and cover letter. To coherently discuss the job and what you have told the organization, you need to be ready. Mr. Jones is certainly ready.

Is it really that important to be at your best for these "couple of questions" over the phone? Make no mistake; what is about to happen as you speak to Mr. Jones is a job interview.

This type of phone interview is a screening interview with a limited scope and time. It is possibly more important than the actual sit-down, in-person interview at his office. If you blow these questions, there will be no further interview. If there are indeed two questions, either one could be a total eliminator.

Mr. Jones has called you because of one or more of the following reasons:

- He has too many candidates to formally interview, and he is trying to cut the list down to a manageable size.
- He is looking for a specific item that may eliminate you – such as involvement in activities he has found to be counterproductive.
- He is looking for specific qualifications not previously mentioned.
- He has seen something in your resume or cover letter that he would like clarified.
- He intends to invite you to a formal interview and is asking qualification or preliminary questions.

Handling the Screening Interview

To be ready for screening interviews such as the one described, you should:

- Stay current on all active applications including requirements and what you have told the hiring organization. Review this information daily, if necessary, to keep it in focus.
- Keep all information on each job together in a folder or clipped/stapled and make sure it is handy

229

to refer to if you are contacted for a screening interview.

- Be prepared to do this if caught unprepared: tell the caller that you cannot talk right then but will be glad to call her back in 5 or 10 minutes. Then quickly prepare and get into a good positive frame of mind and call back.

The Formal Phone Interview

The formal phone interview is usually arranged beforehand for a specific time. It is similar to the face-to-face interview but is on the phone. There may be one or multiple interviewers; there is probably a prepared list of questions; and most other conditions apply. To prepare for this type of interview, review Chapters 17 through 21, plus the following points:

- Arrange to be in a quiet comfortable place, alone, to receive the call and participate in the interview.
- Arrange to have no interruptions and allow none.
- Dress as you would for a face-to-face interview. Without going into great detail, trust me that this is important. It gives you confidence and puts you in the proper frame of mind.
- Do not use a speakerphone.
- Place all reference materials in good visual position. This should include your resume and cover letter, the job description, and can include

flash cards with important points to make or questions to ask.

• If you know the name(s) of the interviewer(s) place this in view for reference.

Keep in mind that the only communication you have at your disposal is the sound of your voice. From this the interviewer will assume other things. Your body language cannot be seen nor your facial expressions.

If you are smiling, this must come across the phone line. Do not make any gestures or facial gestures you would not make face-to-face. Keep smiling and maintain good posture. It is truly amazing how much can be picked up on the phone by an alert interviewer.

Follow-up is equally important if not more so for the phone interview than in a face-to-face meeting. A thank you letter should go out immediately reviewing positive points in your favor that came up in the interview.

You can and should practice phone interviews with a helper. Have them call you unexpectedly with a quick couple of tough questions. This will get you more used to this type of thinking quickly in that type of circumstance. Mistakes you make on the practice runs will help you to correct before the real thing.

Speed Tip # 27

Keep all your materials for each application handy to the telephone so you can respond to a screening call quickly and well.

Chapter

23

Dress and Grooming

Half Way There

It has been said of interviewees that if they are properly dressed and groomed, they are half way to a successful interview. I would agree with this view. Grooming shows the interviewer how you feel about the process and the hiring organization. If you have gone to some effort to look businesslike, it shows proper respect.

Considerable research has been done on the effect of clothing on others in given situations. A number of books have been written on the subject, and fashion and grooming consultants are still being retained by firms to ensure that their key people are at their visual best.

Listed here are some suggestions on attire for contact with a hiring organization. This includes not only the interview but other contacts prior to being hired. This could include picking up an application, taking a pre-interview test or dropping off a resume.

- Wear proper business attire. A dress or suit for women and a suit or sports coat and slacks for men. Do not assume that normal dress for the job is best for an interview. Find out what the normal dress is for that position in that organization and dress a little better.

- Men should avoid loud or bright ties. A dark tie with some red or maroon is best.

- Avoid "high fashion" or ultra trendy attire. Dress conservatively and be a bit conservative. You can liven up your clothing if and when you get hired.

- If wearing a suit or dress, a dark color is normally preferred with navy blue being the best. Summer season may dictate a lighter color.

- Men should avoid black shirts or pants. This consistently tests negative.

- Shirts or blouses should be neatly pressed. White is the best color. If in any doubt, get a new shirt or blouse for the occasion.

- Do not wear a hat.

- Men's long hair should be pulled back into a neat pigtail.

- Men should shave all areas of the face not covered by beard, mustache or sideburns.

- Hide any tattoos as much as possible.

235

- Avoid wearing nose, lip, tongue, or eyebrow rings.

- Men should avoid earrings.

- Women should wear only small, conservative earrings, with no more than 2 in each ear.

- Do not smoke, chew tobacco, chew gum, eat, or drink unless offered a drink such as coffee, tea, soda or water and others are drinking.

- Do not wear heavy perfume and do not smoke or be around smoke for 2 hours prior to an interview. Do not smell of smoke.

- Do not carry a briefcase or large purse unless bringing work samples to display. A small portfolio or leather folder is fine. Women should carry small, conservative purses.

- Shoes should be clean or shined, conservative, without large scuff marks.

- Keys or chains should not be hanging from belts.

- Do not wear sunglasses on top of the head or reading glasses on a neck chain.

- Avoid all large or flashy jewelry.

- Avoid high fashion hairstyles.

- Always wear your smile.

- Avoid wearing any buttons or insignia denoting unrelated organizations, political or religious affiliations, sports teams, awards or any such logos or badges.

Your clothing is one of your tools in your job search and in the interview in particular. You cannot expect to craft a good job interview performance without good tools. Tools should be carefully selected and used with intelligence.

In *upper level* executive positions, those interviewing you will have a good knowledge of fine, expensive clothing. Something off the bargain rack may look good to you; but if you expect to move into this level, you must dress the part. This means several top quality outfits for the series of interviews you can expect for senior positions.

An experienced senior executive can spot an inexpensive suit from across the room instantly. Do not skimp here if you are after a senior position. Get

237

help if you need it, but ensure that you are well coordinated, elegant, and expensively attired.

Chapter

24

Research on the Organization and Interviewer

Knowledge is Power

Going into a job interview is difficult enough without being hampered by the lack of facts about the hiring. There is no question that the more knowledge you have about the hiring organization and the interviewer the better your situation. Specific knowledge can enable you to speak on current hot topics, avoid dangerous areas, and understand the dynamics that created the opening.

Areas of information on the hiring organiza tion that you can use in your application and interviewing process:

- **Corporate ownership.** If it is a private, non-governmental organization, who actually owns it? Is it a subsidiary of a subsidiary of a subsidiary of a global corporation or does a single person own it or something in between? Is it or could it be the target of a takeover? This can make a difference if the current or potential corporate parent has strongly-held views on a topic you will be discussing in the interview.

- **Organizational structure.** Where does the position you are applying for fit into the structure? Where does your boss fit in? Is the position in a department, division or section that makes sense to

240

you? How did this opening happen? Was someone fired, or did they quit and why? Is a reorganization imminent? This information can also indicate a possible career path or a lack of one for you.

- **Power dynamics and politics.** Does your potential boss have the influence to protect you in difficult situations? Is your potential boss or department in or out of favor with senior management? Will you be able to accomplish what is expected or will internal political influence block your efforts?

- **Organizational vision and philosophy.** Where is the organization going, and what is it trying to do? How does it feel about issues relative to the industry, to its mission, and all the way to your position?

- **Organizational reputation** Is the organization respected? Does it have a solid ethical history or is it in the middle of ethical controversy? What has it done in the past relative to its employees, customers or competitors?

- **Current events.** What are the hot issues that are affecting the organization right now? How do they relate to your potential position now and in the future? What is happening in the industry that the organization is for or against and why?

Here are some pieces of information that would help you in understanding the dynamics of your interview. This is information about the person or persons who will be conducting the interview(s).

- Who is the interviewer? (Name & title)

- Is the interviewer an employee of the hiring organization or a contract interviewer?

- Would this person be your boss or be in your chain of command?

- Is the interviewer a new or long term employee? How long has the person been in this position?

- What are this person's feelings about the issues concerning the position you are applying for? Is this a "by the book" manager or a laid-back staff executive?

- What are the goals of the interviewer in conducting the interview? Is this an initial screening interview, an information gathering interview or an interview to narrow the list down to the final candidates?

242

- What is the interviewer's reputation and standing in the organization?

Research Data Sources

In order to obtain and thereby use the information outlined here, you need to have sources. The following are sources that can supply this type of information.

- **Library**. Libraries contain considerable information on local, regional, and national organizations. They have listings of companies, trade and other publications, industry executives, and even listings of trade articles by subject. Ask the reference librarian to help you. These people are highly skilled researchers and are generally quite willing to help you.

- **The Internet** Many organizations have their own websites, which contain useful information on themselves. Using search engines, search the name of the organization, their competitors, their products, their industry, and subjects of interest to them.

- **Trade Magazines**. Find the magazines, newsletters, and journals of the industry in which

243

the hiring organization belongs. They may have informative articles which can help you. Some of these are on line on the Internet.

- **Local Newspaper Files.** Some newspaper files can be searched by keyword on computers at the newspaper. Look for the organization in these files back up to two years.

- **Annual Report.** If the organization publishes an annual report, it will have a lot of useful data, such as financial reports, earnings, organizational and individual accomplishments, and plans for the future. Some libraries carry these or you can ask the organization itself.

- **Executive Listings.** Listings like "Who's Who" in various industries and trade publications can supply personal information on key people in many organizations.

- **Public Relations Department of the Organization.** They can supply a surprising amount of information. If possible, ask for an informational interview with an organization executive. This can be extremely helpful.

244

- **Unions.** For organizations that have union contracts, those unions can often have interesting information from a different angle than the organization.

- **Customers.** Those served by the organization in some way can tell you things about their operations and character. Customers are often quite willing to tell you what they think of an organization, both positive and negative.

- **Alumni Associations.** If you are a graduate of a college or university, you can check with them to see if another alumna perhaps works for the organization. When it comes to helping a former classmate, old school ties can be stronger than you might realize. This inside source can supply you with valuable data you cannot obtain elsewhere.

- **Research Services.** Research companies can do a lot of research for you in many areas if you are willing to pay for the service. If it is a high level job and you have limited time, it may well be worth it to you.

Many other information sources are available, limited only by your imagination, creativity, and perseverance. If it seems like real work, it is. Is the position worth your effort? It probably is, or you

245

would not be pursuing this type of position in the first place. The long-term benefit can vastly outweigh the short-term effort. This type of research can be of major benefit after landing the job. If you are not hired there, it can be of benefit on another job quest in the same field.

Section Six

Six

Post Contact

The Accelerated Job Search

Chapter

25

Follow-up

Maintaining Momentum

After each interview, a letter should go out as soon as possible from you to the interviewer or interviewers. As basic elements, it should contain the following:

- A sincere thank you for the consideration extended to you by both granting and conducting the interview.

- A review of the points covered or discussed that were most favorable to you. These most typically would be a situation in the interview where you were asked if you had specific experience, and you had responded that you had excellent experience in that area.

Perhaps you were asked if you knew the work of Dr. John Smith and you related that you had studied under Dr. Smith, personally for two years. These types of positive highlights should be mentioned.

"It was a pleasure reviewing with you the highly rewarding time that I spent studying with Dr. Smith."

"I felt that my experience with the spray metal process fit well with your requirements."

250

- A confident line about moving forward, such as: "I look forward to continuing with the selection process."

- Perhaps a line about how comfortable you felt in discussing the opportunity and that you had a good feeling about the position and the people. (If indeed this was true.)

Accuracy

To ensure that the letter is accurately sent, try to obtain a business card of the interviewer before you leave the interview. Failing this, ask a receptionist for the exact address to send the interviewer a thank you note. This is critical to ensuring that it gets there and to demonstrate that you get your details straight.

Take some notes of key details as soon as you leave the interview room to give yourself maximum fresh recall of the important points. Waiting until you arrive home may cause you to forget one or more of the points you would want to emphasize in a follow-up thank you letter.

Proof read this letter as carefully or more so than your original resume and cover letter. Poor grammar or punctuation in this letter may be worse than sending no letter at all. Have another person look at it to be sure.

Speed Tip # 28

Prepare a draft of the thank you letter before the interview. Then fill in key details afterwards and get it on its way back to the interviewer as soon as possible.

Chapter

26

The Offer – Negotiating Terms

One More Step

You have been unemployed for a few weeks or a few months. You do not like being unemployed and have put all your efforts into being again employed.

You have been in a state of suspense and anxiety all through the selection process. Your focus has been on winning the contest with other applicants and *getting the job*. A lot has gone through your mind. Will they hire me or will they not? Do they think I am the best candidate? Do they want me?

If you have gone through the process before, perhaps several times, and not been selected, you can be forgiven for focusing solely on getting a job offer. The offer has been your end game.

The phone rings, and it is the hiring manager at the organization where you have been undergoing the selection process. He exchanges pleasantries and then comes what you have been waiting for – an offer of employment. You have succeeded in your quest. It is all over but the details. But is it?

The offer (which could also come by mail or in person) includes a stated starting salary. You are excited and grateful for the offer and certainly do not want to offend the wonderful person who is giving you this great new opportunity. The salary offered is a little below what you would have hoped for, but you certainly do not want to seem ungrateful and get off on the wrong foot.

Even worse, it could blow the whole deal and they might withdraw their offer if you mentioned that it was a little low right now. Perhaps after a few months on the job, when they see how valuable you really are would be a good time to bring up the subject of a higher salary.

The Driver's Seat

It is natural to think all these things, but stop. You could not be more wrong. The period of your career with this new organization when you have absolute maximum leverage is the point between the offer and the acceptance. This period may last a few seconds or up to a week in some cases. It is the time where they have said, "We want you", and you have not yet agreed to terms.

This is the time to state what you want. They are not likely to be offended and withdraw the offer, but they are likely to give credence to what you have to say. If you state a higher figure and they cannot or will not meet it, suggest a compromise or perhaps an increase in benefits or a concession on working conditions. If you wait a month or two after you have started the job, you will find that your leverage has fallen to near zero. Do it now. It is your best shot.

Pre-Offer Feelers

Some employers, during the interview process, may try to get a sense of your feelings on salary. You may hear:

- "So, what are your salary requirements?"
- "Do you have a salary figure in mind?"
- "What are you going to need to make?"

These, of course, are attempts to get you to be the first to throw out a figure. If you do, you may be too low or too high. Try to avoid a direct response. Something like, "That's certainly a good question. Can you tell me the range for this position?" is a good counter to get them to speak first.

Yes, it is a game, but a very important game to you. Give it some thought before the offer gets to you, and you will be far better prepared when the time comes.

Chapter

27

Starting and Keeping the Job

Starting Off

Starting a new job can be like the first day in a new school. It may be a little scary, intimidating, and unclear as to what your role is or will be. It is an excellent opportunity to make a lasting impression on your new co-workers. Will it be a good or bad one?

There are certain tendencies of brand new employees everywhere. These may include:

- To want to know where the restroom and break facilities are, and the safety and security conditions.
- To want to talk about themselves to establish their credibility as an experienced person.
- To want to fit in.
- To want to make a good impression.

These tendencies often get new employees off to a bad start in the eyes of their new co-workers. They try too hard, talk about themselves too much, and often tell "how we did it at ...." when their new colleagues really do not want to hear it.

They want the new employee to start conforming to the way they are familiar with. The larger and more formal the organization, the more this is true. Use of uniforms or other similar clothing promotes this type of feeling.

To avoid problems as you start off on a new job, some suggestions would be:

- Be friendly, positive, and accepting of new things.
- Find out who does what and respect their roles.
- Do not volunteer too much about how it was done somewhere else.
- Be patient.
- Listen well before expressing an opinion or suggesting changes.
- Find out what the truly important things are in the job and focus on those things.
- Be a trusted person.
- Do not panic. Things usually look better and less overwhelming after the first few days.

Continuing in the Job

After you have settled in, you need to concentrate on more long term aspects of the job in order to keep it. This is a great concept. It tends to help avoid unemployment. Some points to keep in mind:

- Keeping your boss comfortable in relation to you is the single most effective job maintenance technique you can employ. Doing things that make your boss uncomfortable or unhappy is not a good way to ensure long term employment.

- Be a team player. Think of ways to assist others.
- Become valuable to the organization.
- Stay flexible.
- Cross-train, if possible.
- Think of ways to match your own goals with that of the organization.
- Constantly learn.

Work Long and Prosper

Working for many years at one place is not as popular as it once was, but it still holds many advantages. Seniority, raises, better benefits and retirement are things that some organizations can provide long term. Besides, unemployment is no fun, right?

Section Seven

Your Positive Future

The Accelerated Job Search

Chapter

28

Attitude – Maintaining it for Your Job and Your Life

A Valuable Asset

Your attitude is the guiding light of your personality, confidence, stress level, and future. Everything that happens to you and everything that comes from you is filtered through your attitude. It guides how you handle yourself and determines to a large part how well you do on your job.

Termination of employees happens far more often for a failure of attitude than it does for a failure of competence. On the other end, getting promoted often depends on a display of positive and confident attitude. Job assignments, performance appraisals, recognition, and reputation all are affected by your attitude. A successful working career is not likely without a good attitude toward the job, co-workers, and yourself.

Raw Power

Positive energy has been proven many times to create and conserve your energy. You can test this yourself. Start a day with a strongly positive attitude and go about some difficult tasks. Somewhere in the midst of your work, allow someone to inject a negative theme into the process. You can physically feel the energy drain from your body. A negative attitude can sap energy, but only in the absence of a source of positive attitude and commitment. Compare it to light and darkness. In the presence of light, darkness moves back; but when the light goes out, darkness moves in swiftly and surely.

To create and maintain the power of a positive attitude (light over darkness), you must first decide that you will develop and maintain a positive feeling about all that you do. To have a positive attitude at work, you must develop it for your life. You are the same person at work and away.

There are many methods, books, courses, trainers, and tactics for gaining and keeping a positive attitude. There are too many to list here; but at the risk of seeming overly simplistic, I would like to share one method with you that I have seen to have success.

A Series of Small Victories

To realize the major victory of a positive attitude and a positive life, you must put the pieces of it together. Consider everything that you do during your day as a challenge, large or small. The small challenges, like walking across the room, you may take no normal notice of; but for some in this world, your small hurdles are enormous challenges. Learn to appreciate what you can do, and understand that not everyone can do them.

265

Therefore, as you conquer these small hurdles such as getting dressed, getting a meal, reading a paper, driving a car, having a conversation, or some of thousands of other things, consider each one successfully done a victory. As the day progresses, you will pile up many victories as you successfully complete many small things.

Realize that these victories are a positive force in your life; and, therefore, see the positive light in them that drives back the darkness of negativity and despair. From the series of these small victories, you can then clearly see the large victory that your life truly is.

Keep this positive force in focus in your life and your work, and you will gain the confidence that your future will be positive also.

INDEX

269

The Accelerated Job Search

*To order books and courses
on this and other subjects, contact:*

The Management Advantage, Inc.
P.O. Box 3708
Walnut Creek, CA 94598-0708
Voice: (925) 671-0404
FAX: (925) 825-3930
E-mail: tmainc@management-advantage.com
Website: //www.management-advantage.com

**Proudly serving management and
human resource professionals
since 1987.**

- *Publications*
- *Products*
- *Training*
- *Consulting*

The Accelerated Job Search

x